THE PACIFIC
COOKBOOK

THE PACIFIC COOKBOOK

Compiled by
Rene Jansen

SUMMIT BOOKS
Sydney · Auckland · London · New York

Acknowledgements
Air New Zealand gratefully thank the following for
their assistance: Rees Designstore; Walker and Hall
Ltd.; Arts Delight; Consulate of Samoa; Island Arts
Shop, Samoa House; Mrs Marie Ewbank of East
West Antiques; Asahi Japanese Centre, Simon Kan;
Peter Aldridge and Peter Furstensteiner.

Published by Summit Books
176 South Creek Road,
Dee Why West,
NSW Australia 2099.

1st Edition 1980
First published by Lansdowne Press New Zealand
as a special edition for

© Lansdowne Press, 1980

Typeset in New Zealand by Auckland Typographical Services

Printed by Toppan Printing Co. (Singapore) (Pte) Limited
38 Liu Fang Road, Jurong, Singapore 22

Designer, Leonard Cobb
Photographer, Desmond Williams

National Library of Australia Cataloguing-In-Publication Data

The Pacific cookbook.

Index
ISBN 0 7271 0520 5

1. Cookery. I. Jansen, Rene, comp.

641.5

Cover photograph, Kokoda and Chicken in Pineapple

CONTENTS

INTRODUCTION
By John McDermott

Food is a universal language and a country's cuisine is an immediate and pleasurable way of appreciating a new culture, a means of understanding the origin and evolution of a life style, a way of identifying cultural relationships and influences.

While geographically separated, the countries represented share a common boundary – the Pacific Ocean – the source of many of the exotic dishes presented in this book. Each country has created its own special flavours, sometimes marrying the tastes of local and imported cuisines, sometimes inventing its own unique specialities, but always providing delights for the adventurous gourmet.

HAWAII

The islands of Hawaii have changed from pre-war somnolent islands devoted to sugar cane and pineapple to modern destination resorts designed for visiting sunseekers.

Waikiki, once only reached by the Matson fleet, *was* the 'Pink Palace', the Royal Hawaiian Hotel and the old Moana with the Outrigger Canoe Club sandwiched in between.

Today Waikiki is vibrant. Bound by the Ala Wai Canal and Diamond Head, it affords the visitor every cosmopolitan facility for every ethnic appetite, discos, cinemas, fast-food operations and shopping complexes. And, of course, fine beaches.

Gastronomically, the Hawaiian Islands have an appeal all their own. Fresh pineapple, macadamia nut ice-cream in papaya (paw-paw) and the magnificent *luau* with pork, fruit and vegetables cooked in an underground pit, are all irresistible specialities. With a large Japanese and Chinese population there are genuine tea houses and sushi or teppan bars catering to the local citizens and a thousand Chinese restaurants specialising in Mandarin, Shanghai, Schezwann foods. The outstanding Chinese chefs are nomadic and their devotees follow them any place!

You will taste the best of Hawaii, in our opinion, if you go with a resident who has pre-ordered a Chinese meal.

Italian, French, Vietnamese, Filipino, Korean, Mexican, Portuguese, Greek and Jewish cuisines extend the Hawaiian menu to provide a truly pleasurable eating experience.

SAMOA

American Samoa consists of seven islands which have been under the jurisdiction of the United States since 1900. The principal island, Tutuila, with a population of 30,000 boasts of a territorial museum, a cable car ride to the top of Solo Hill, scenic island trips and a handicraft centre offering tapa print materials, woven baskets and shell necklaces.

Western Samoa consists primarily of the populous islands of Savai'i and Upolu. In the 19th century the islands were claimed by the Germans who lost their territorial rights in the first World War and the governing of the islands was given to New Zealand in 1920.

The Samoans are the original Polynesians. It is believed that the island of Savai'i was populated around 500 B.C., probably by dark Fijians who over hundreds of years developed new characteristics and a language and, after migrating to Marquesas, became the tall, golden, 'Eastern Polynesians'. The present day Samoans are genuinely friendly and deeply religious, whether Protestant or Catholic.

Local customs and family ties are equally strong, the land affording the central bond. The traditional feast, the *fiafia*, offers an opportunity to sample the delicious tropical fruits and the most popular dish, pulusami, taro leaves cooked in coconut cream. You do not eat while standing or when walking through a village. Traditionally the rules of hospitality forbid a visitor to speak to his Samoan host while standing. You sit either with your legs crossed or you cover your outstretched legs with a mat.

FIJI

Fiji comprises hundreds of islands filled with smiles and when a Fijian greets you with a loud 'Bula' the sun shines everywhere.

To the winter-weary visitor, Fiji and its many islands offer unique opportunities to recover, relax and enjoy.

Suva itself is a small city-state. Capital of the country, with a population over 100,000, it boasts of duty-free shops, markets, restaurants and private clubs.

It is immediately apparent in Fiji that the land is devoted to sugar cane – a product primarily grown by Indians who were brought to Fiji as indentured field workers in the latter part of the 19th century.

However, the Fijians still retain 82 per cent ownership of the land and with it they retain 82 per cent of their culture. It is not obvious to the visitor in the beginning but the longer one stays in Fiji the more one learns to appreciate the retention of the family-tribe culture.

North of Viti Levu is Vanua Levu where you can stay at Namale Plantation and share in the life of a remote coconut plantation.

Next to Vanua Levu is the garden island of Taveuni and off-shore outstanding underwater viewing of fish and coral formations.

Visitors should also spend a day on Fiji's first capital city of Levuka on the island of Ovalau.

Also outside of Suva, easily reached by boat, is the exclusive island of Toberua, a jewel of a resort.

Desirable but difficult to visit is the Coral Coast island of Beqa, home of the famous Fijian firewalkers.

The food in Fiji covers a broad spectrum. Local, cooked-in-the-pit Fijian food is varied: pig, fish, fruit. Distinctive is *duruka,* a pre-flower sprout from wild sugar cane that looks and tastes like asparagus, only sweeter.

There is good Chinese cooking, and the Indian cooking? Ah, yes! The subtle differences in the many types of curries and the many exotic flavours delight the discerning palate.

Fiji Bitter is the local beer brewed by Carlton Breweries in Lautoka. The other common drink is *kava* or *yaqona* or *grog* which is a mild stunner made from the root of the pepper plant. Try it. After all, travel should be an experience of new places and new things . . . and Fiji has many new experiences to offer.

TAHITI

Tahiti is an island of many charms and is only one island of hundreds in all of French Polynesia. The farther you get away from Tahiti, the smaller the population and the more languid the pace. Time is not measured in minutes or hours but in days and weeks.

Papeete is the 'Paris of the Pacific'. The Sunday morning pre-dawn market place is one of the great weekly events in the South Pacific where the visitor can participate in true street drama and mingle with Chinese, French and Polynesians sauntering through sheds crammed with fresh fish, garden vegetables, exotic fruits, and delicacies of the kitchen. (After the Sunday market the locals go to the *Au Delice* bakery behind the Catholic cathedral and buy flaky croissants, still hot, and take them home to eat with fresh melon from the island of Huahine.)

The famous peaks and bays of Moorea are only seven air minutes from Tahiti. Relaxed. Uncrowded.

The Leeward Group (called in French 'les isles sous le vent') of the Society Group include Bora Bora, Huahine and Raiatea, all exotic playgrounds northwest of Tahiti.

Further north are the low-lying, white-sand atolls of the Tuamotus with vast lagoons, pearl divers and glorious swimming.

Beyond the Tuamotus are the mysterious Marquesas, rugged, reefless, adventure-calling, and to the south of Tahiti are the Australs where visitors can be counted on one hand.

One thing that all islands have in common is outstanding food, an intermarriage of Polynesian, Chinese and French cuisines. The visitor benefits. Nowhere else in the South Pacific is there such a selection of outstanding restaurants or choice of food in the markets.

Two Polynesian foods that will haunt you are properly cooked breadfruit, with its pungent odour, and the Polynesian dessert, *poki* – pronounced 'po-kee' – a pudding made of fresh fruit and tapioca powder and when served warm covered with coconut cream is one of the finest (and fattening) desserts we have ever tasted.

Every vintage of French wine is available. Even the Algerian table wines seem smoother in French Polynesia, and the local beer is very satisfactory. French Polynesia is an exotic land and its food an exquisite complement.

AUSTRALIA

The breadth of the country is awe-inspiring and challenging.

The Great Barrier Reef, the world's largest chain of coral formations; the many islands; Cape York Peninsula on a bush pilot's tour; Darwin with safaris into the bush; Broome, a snorting, kicking frontier town on the northwest coast; Alice Springs and Ayers Rock. Then in complete contrast, the ski resorts of Thredbo and Mt. Buller. The finale is an Australian Rules Football game in Melbourne.

A country of diversity: in scenery and adventure. See the famous Melbourne Cup, the vineyards on Hunter Valley and Barossa Valley, two of but a dozen well-known Australian vineyards, or take a houseboat up the River Murray.

High on the list is a visit to the underground world of Coober Pedy where everyone avoids the heat by living beneath the surface of the land and where 90 per cent of the famous Australian opals are mined.

Go to an Australian country horse meet. Drive across the Nullarbor Plain to the gold mining town of Kalgoorlie. Visit lovely Perth on the west coast and sunbathe on its golden beaches.

Catch an opera in the Sydney Opera House or spend an entire month motoring back and forth through beautiful Tasmania, perhaps squandering a dollar or two at the casino in Hobart.

See a beach carnival at Bondi and tramp through the hills of the Blue Mountains and Kosciusko National Park and water ski on the Gold Coast.

There are now fourteen million people in Australia, a country the size of the United States, and they are open, friendly, no-nonsense people. A new element has been added since the war, the arrival of thousands of Europeans. Italian and Greek and other European languages are heard in the street with increasing frequency. The result can be seen in the many excellent ethnic restaurants.

NEW ZEALAND

The country is so beautiful. Jewel lakes tucked away in remote corners, beaches, bays, quiet inlets, roaring surf. In contrast to the many aquatic scenes are the high mountains . . . snow-capped, wrapped in blankets of green trees. In between the ocean and the mountain peaks are the vast hectares of fields, vibrant in spring with lawn colours, sprinkled with white sheep and dotted with fat cattle.

Whether swimming, surfing, snowskiing, mountaineering or just relaxing, the visitor to New Zealand experiences the scenic wealth and beauty of a land whose smallness belies its diversity.

Pound for pound, New Zealand must provide the best larder in the Pacific. The lamb and the beef, as you would expect of an agrarian society, are first rate.

For the gourmet with a love of sea food, the Bluff oysters, the Nelson scallops and the Napier lobsters exemplify the bounty of New Zealand waters. Fresh fruits are everywhere and frequently exotic.

Besides excellent breweries, New Zealand has an extensive wine industry increasing in quantity while improving in quality.

Restaurants in New Zealand, too, keep increasing in number and variety, offering such delicacies as freshly caught trout broiled with a cover of butter and flecks of onion and tomato, followed by a dessert of tamarillo over dairy-rich ice cream.

THE UNITED STATES

When you fly over the United States on a clear day, you are amazed at its vastness and variety. The West Coast is a nation unto itself, from the bays at San Diego to the healthy shores of Seattle. You roll inland over Las Vegas and Reno, past Phoenix and the Grand Canyon to the Rockies, Aspen, ski fields and trout streams, and down the other side to the vast, rich plains of wheatfields and cornfields flanked on the north by the Great Lakes and to the south by Texas and longhorn cattle and the French touch in New Orleans.

At the extreme south, there is Miami in Spanish-influenced Florida and then north through the tobacco country of the Carolinas and the Virginias to Washington D.C.

North to Boston and Cape Cod, the land of the Kennedys, cradle of the Revolution, now a centre for learning and medical expertise.

Farther north to the word-sparse, tree-rich hills of the Vermont and New Hampshire farmers and then to the crashing coasts of Maine.

The hardy, twangy New Englander with his British backbone, the Irish of Boston and the Jews, Italians and Puerto Ricans of New York, the Swedes of Minnesota and Wisconsin, the Mexicans of the border, the Chinese who came with the California gold rush, the Scandanavian lumberjacks of Puget Sound, the Japanese farmers . . . for over 200 years the world poured into the United States.

Still the pride of roots remains and there is new strength in the heritage of mother countries which is reflected in festivals and language and in cooking.

There is San Francisco crab and Alaska crab and Chesapeake Bay crab. There are turnip greens and black peas and Dewberry pie in the south and chilli con carne in El Paso and New England boiled dinners. The beef steaks are measured by centimetres in Kansas City and the salmon steaks are measured by the tonne out west in the state of Washington.

I recall a pigeon baked in a bed of noodles and tomatoes sent over by an Italian friend in Santa Clara and a cold caviar pie created by a Russian cousin in the foothills of Los Angeles.

The sheer size and colour of the United States thumbs its nose at a short description.

You must see it . . . and taste it . . . piece by piece, region by region yourself.

HONG KONG

Hong Kong is probably the most fascinating city in the world.

Visually it is stunning. Skyscraping office buildings, hotels and multi-level shopping malls hem in Victoria Harbour which is like a bath tub filled with floating buoys: scrambling junks, white yachts, grey battleships, freighters, cruise liners, hydrofoils heading for Macao, Star Ferries shuttling back and forth between Kowloon Peninsula and Hong Kong Island.

Over four million people now live within the tight confines of the British Crown Colony of Hong Kong. A tour of Hong Kong can encompass the walled city of Kam Tin in the New Territories, the Tiger Balm Gardens behind Causeway Bay with grotesque but humourously fascinating statues of animals and plastic scenes of Chinese mythology, and the floating city of Aberdeen.

Food in Hong Kong is predominantly Chinese and each region has evolved its own style: Cantonese, Shanghai, Peking, Honan, Schezwann. Cantonese, perhaps the best known, is mild. Shanghai is famous for fish preparation. Honan for sweet and sour. Peking for its crispy duck and Schezwann its north-of-the-border spiciness. Russian, Japanese, Indian and Malayan foods add to the rich and irresistible banquet presented by Hong Kong.

SINGAPORE

Singapore is a captivating Oriental city and has rapidly become the commercial centre of South East Asia.

The city is not Chinese although two-thirds of its citizens are. It is not British although much of its heritage is. Its basic Malay background and its large Indian population are reflected in its personality. The character of Singapore may be commercial but its food truly reflects its cultural diversity.

The best food in Singapore is Chinese. However, there are exciting local dishes. *Satay* can hardly be avoided. Pieces of meat barbecued on a skewer and dipped in tangy peanut or spiced pineapple dip sauce and served as hors d'oeuvres or as a main dish at streetside food stalls or Indonesian restaurants.

The 'steamboat' is like the Japanese *shabu-shabu*. The principle is the same. In Singapore not only meat but seafood and chicken are added to the presentation which you cook yourself in a cauldron of bubbling broth. Restaurants specialise in this main dish along with famous Hainan chicken rice, and with the addition of Malay and Indian curries food in Singapore becomes irresistible.

ENTREES

FILLED AVOCADOS

2 avocados, halved and stoned
1 tomato, diced
1 teaspoon mayonnaise
1 teaspoon cream
1 teaspoon cognac or brandy
1 teaspoon capers
1 or 2 tablespoons Emmenthal or
  young cheese, grated

Remove some of the flesh from the avocado halves, leaving a 'lining' about 5mm deep. Dice the flesh removed. Mix mayonnaise, cream and cognac together and use this dressing to bind the avocado, tomato, and capers together. Divide mixture equally and fill the 4 half avocados. Chill in the refrigerator for about 30 minutes. Serve sprinkled with cheese. Serves 4.

AVOCADO WITH RAVIGOTE MAYONNAISE

2 avocados
120g crabmeat
ravigote mayonnaise
1 tomato fan
2 lemon twists
2 eggs, sliced
parsley

Prepare avocados as above. Mix crabmeat with ravigote mayonnaise and use a quarter of the mixture to fill each avocado half. Garnish as shown in the photograph (p97). Serves 4.

CURRIED MUSSELS

2 tablespoons butter
2 onions, sliced
½ tablespoon flour
½ teaspoon curry
24 mussels
salt and pepper

Melt butter, add onions and brown. Stir in flour, curry and enough water to mix smoothly. Add mussels and a little more water so that mussels are just covered. Season and simmer for 30 minutes. Serves 6.

MUSSELS IN WHITE SAUCE

24 mussels
1 onion, chopped
chopped parsley
2 cups white sauce

Shell mussels. Cook onion in a little water until tender. Add mussels, onion and parsley to sauce and serve. Serves 6.

MUSSELS SOUTHLAND STYLE

150ml dry white wine
1 tablespoon celery, chopped
½ teaspoon sage
6 white peppercorns, crushed
1 teaspoon salt
2.5-3kg cleaned fresh mussels
120g butter
1 tablespoon chives, chopped
1 tablespoon parsley, chopped
2 tablespoons celery salt
1 clove garlic, crushed
120ml cream
2 egg yolks
salt to taste
½ teaspoon curry powder

In a large pot bring to the boil the white wine, celery, sage, peppercorns and salt. Add mussels, cover, and shake pot during cooking to loosen mussels from their shells – about 10 minutes. Remove mussels from pot and shell. Set aside and keep warm. Cream butter with chives, parsley, celery salt and garlic. Grease an ovenproof dish with mixture. Place mussels in serving dish. Beat cream, egg yolks, salt and curry powder to medium thickness. Spread over mussels and place in a very hot oven until top of sauce starts to brown. Serves 4-5.

COCKLE, PIPI OR TUA TUA FRITTERS

24 shellfish
2 eggs, beaten
3 tablespoon flour
1 teaspoon baking powder
pinch of salt
milk (if needed)
lemon juice

Steam shellfish in a colander over a pot of boiling water (do not allow to touch water). Steam until shells open. Beat eggs into flour, baking powder and salt. Add a little milk if mixture too stiff. Remove shellfish from shells and coat in batter mixture. Fry in hot fat. Serve with lemon juice. Serves 4.

TASTY TOHEROA SPECIAL

2 tablespoons butter
1 onion, chopped
3 cups toheroas, minced
2 tablespoons flour
1 teaspoon curry powder
salt and pepper
½ teaspoon mustard
1 tablespoon lemon juice
1 cup water
300ml milk
2 tablespoons parsley, chopped

Melt butter, brown onion, add toheroas and simmer for 10 minutes. Add flour, curry powder, seasoning, mustard and lemon juice and simmer for 5 minutes. Add milk slowly, stirring constantly. If too thick add water. Add parsley and serve on hot toast. Serves 4.

LOBSTER PACIFICA

375g lobster meat, chopped
2 pawpaws, halved
½ cup pineapple pieces
10 melon balls
grapes, halved
2 lemons
parsley
4 lettuce leaves
1 kiwifruit

Marinate lobster in remoulade dressing. Scoop out centre of pawpaws and chop up, keep 'shell'. Mix pawpaw with pineapple, melon and grapes into lobster mixture. Place lettuce leaves inside pawpaw shells, fill with mixture. Garnish with lobster claws, lemon crowns, parsley and sliced kiwifruit. Serves 4.

BLUFF OYSTERS À LA MAISON

½ cup thick cream sauce
2 tablespoons raw spinach, finely
   chopped
1 green onion, finely chopped
4 teaspoons Parmesan cheese,
   grated
2 tablespoons dry white wine
salt and pepper
2 egg yolks
6 oysters and their half-shells
3 tablespoons melted butter
1 lemon, quartered

Place cream sauce in pan and add spinach, green onion, 1 teaspoon grated cheese, white wine and salt and pepper to taste. Bring to boil, stirring constantly. Remove from heat. Beat egg yolks with a few tablespoons of the hot sauce then add to sauce in pan, stirring constantly over a high heat. Place oyster shells upright in a dish and set oysters in their shells. Heap sauce over each oyster, sprinkle rest of grated cheese on top and brush with melted butter. Bake in a very hot oven until golden brown. Serve with lemon quarters. Serves 1.

OYSTER COCKTAIL

24 oysters
cream
parsley

For sauce:
2 tablespoons tomato sauce
1 tablespoon Worcestershire
   sauce
1 tablespoon vinegar
2 tablespoons lemon juice
½ teaspoon salt
2 drops Tabasco sauce

Drain, beard and chop oysters. Combine sauce ingredients and add oysters. Divide into cocktail glasses and top with a dab of unsweetened whipped cream and sprig of parsley. Serves 4-6.

SHELLFISH COCKTAIL

400-500g raw shellfish (oysters,
   scallops, small tender mussels
   and crayfish)
100ml white wine
1 piece lemon peel
1 bay leaf
1 teaspoon salt
5 peppercorns
½ onion, chopped coarsely
lettuce leaves
oysters for garnish
dill
lemon
For sauce:
2 small shallots
1 small garlic clove
1 teaspoon green peppercorns
1 teaspoon Worcestershire sauce
1 teaspoon curry powder
3 tablespoons tomato sauce
250ml mayonnaise
pinch of salt

Steam scallops, mussels and crayfish pieces with wine, bay leaf, lemon peel, salt, peppercorns and onion. Let fish cool in cooking liquid. When cold remove seafood and drain well. Slice scallops.
Prepare following sauce: Chop shallots, garlic and green peppercorns very finely. Add Worcestershire sauce, curry and tomato sauce. Mix well and add mayonnaise and salt. Beat until well blended. Arrange cooked seafood on leaf of lettuce, spoon sauce over and garnish with raw oysters, sprig of dill and lemon wedge. Serves 4-6.

OCTOPUS FRITTERS

1 octopus
oil

For batter:
2 eggs
6 tablespoons flour
2 teaspoons salt
2 teaspoons sherry

Cut out cylindrical envelope of flesh and remove tooth and translucent pen from the octopus. Turn body inside out and cut out the inside, being careful not to puncture the ink sac. The head is discarded. Wash well and cut into 4cm slices. Prepare a batter by beating eggs with flour, salt and sherry. Dip pieces of octopus into batter and then deep fry in very hot oil until golden brown. Drain on absorbent paper and keep hot until ready to serve. Serves 4.
Optional: Octopus marinated in milk and lemon juice for 6-8 hours will be more tender. Drain well before dipping in batter.

CRAYFISH WITH FRUIT

350-400g cooked crayfish
80g melon balls
60g peeled and seeded grapes
60g pineapple
200ml mayonnaise
2 tablespoons cognac
pinch of cayenne pepper
3 tablespoons tomato sauce
1 tablespoon lemon juice
salt
6 lettuce leaves
1 kiwifruit
6 crayfish legs
6 lemon wedges
parsley

Dice crayfish and mix in with all fruit. Prepare sauce with mayonnaise, cognac, pepper, tomato sauce, lemon juice and salt. Pour over crayfish and fruit, mix gently. Arrange on lettuce leaves in cocktail glasses and garnish with slices of kiwifruit and crayfish legs, lemon wedges and parsley. Serves 6.

KIWI COCKTAIL

4 kiwifruit
200g shrimps
1 small can mandarins and 2
    tablespoons of the juice
pinch of ginger
juice of half a lemon

Peel kiwifruit and slice. Wash and drain shrimps. Mix mandarins, kiwifruit, shrimps and ginger together and place in cocktail glasses. Mix mandarin juice and lemon together and use as sauce. Chill before serving. Serves 4-6.

KOKODA – (RAW FISH IN COCONUT CREAM)

750g fish (snapper or mullet)
salt
1 cup lemon or lime juice
1 cup thick coconut cream
green onion or tomato for garnish

Cut fish fillets into 1cm pieces. Sprinkle with salt and leave a few minutes. Pour over lemon juice – the fish must be just covered by juice. Leave 2-3 hours, or overnight in the refrigerator, until the fish is white. (The time taken to 'whiten' depends on the kind of fish and the acidity of the lemons or limes. Cooling slows down the process.) Strain off juice and squeeze out moisture by pressing in a strainer.
Prepare coconut cream (see index) and pour over the fish. Garnish with chopped green onion or tomato. Serve well chilled. Serves 4-6.

REEF PANCAKE

For pancakes:
1 egg
60g flour
1 cup milk
few drops of oil
pinch of salt
pinch of sugar
oil for frying

For filling:
1 medium onion, chopped
butter
130g smoked salmon, chopped
2 hard-boiled eggs, chopped
fresh dill, ground
parsley, chopped
fish sauce

For fish sauce:
40g butter
60g flour
2 tablespoons white wine
1 cup fish stock
30ml cream
3-4 tablespoons hollandaise sauce
parsley

Pancakes: Make up smooth pancake batter from given ingredients and cook very thin pancakes. Set aside.
Filling: Fry onion in a little butter until brown. Add salmon, eggs, herbs and fish sauce and mix well. Let boil once. Spoon mixture into pancakes and roll up. Place on silver serving platter and leave in 180°C oven for a few minutes.
Fish sauce: Make a roux sauce with butter and flour. Add wine and fish stock made by boiling fish bones, 1 bay leaf, 2 cloves and a slice of onion in water for 30 minutes, then remove bones. Reduce sauce for 30 minutes more, add cream and then beat in hollandaise sauce. Pour over pancakes and flash off under grill. Sprinkle with parsley and serve. Serves 4.

MEXICAN FISH

450g fresh mackerel, snapper
  or mullet
salt
6 lemons
260g tomatoes, peeled and
  chopped
1 tablespoon parsley, chopped
1 tablespoon chives, chopped
2 onions, sliced
1 knife-tip cayenne pepper
1 teaspoon salt and pepper
2 tablespoons oil

This is a dish for gourmets who enjoy raw fish dishes. Skin fish, remove fins, cut into small pieces and salt. Squeeze lemons and marinate fish in juice for 12 hours. Pour off juice. Place tomatoes in a bowl and sprinkle with chopped parsley, chives, onion, cayenne and salt and pepper. (Dill leaves can be included.) Top with fish pieces and pour on oil. Serve with dry white bread. Serves 4-6.

SALMON SLICES WITH BÉARNAISE SAUCE

6 x 200g salmon slices
salt and pepper
flour
115g butter
parsley
lemon slices
béarnaise sauce

Season salmon slices with salt and pepper. Sprinkle lightly with flour and brown on both sides in heated butter. Drain and reserve butter. Place in a long dish, garnish with fresh parsley and slices of lemon. Pour the hot butter over the salmon. Serve with béarnaise sauce on the side. Serves 6.

NELSON SCALLOPS À LA PARISIENNE

30 scallops, and shells
½ bottle white wine
duchess potatoes
1 cup mushrooms, sliced
butter

For white wine sauce:
fish stock
roux
juice of ½ a small lemon
140ml cream
salt and pepper

Blanch scallops, simmer in white wine, drain and place in scallop shells. Pipe duchess potatoes around shell and cover scallops with sautéed mushrooms, coat with white wine sauce and glaze under grill.

Make up fish stock by sautéing in a little oil; 500g fish bones, 1 chopped onion, 2-3 chopped leeks, a few peppercorns, ½ bay leaf, ½ teaspoon chopped parsley and 3-4 chopped mushrooms. Sauté lightly, add ½ cup white wine from that used to cook scallops, then 2 cups water. Simmer for 20 minutes. Add strained stock to cooled roux sauce made from 50g flour and 40g butter. Cook for further 25 minutes, add lemon juice, cream and seasoning. Serves 6.

SCALLOPS SAUTÉED WITH GARLIC BUTTER SAUCE

450g whole scallops cut into
    12mm slices
salt
white pepper
flour
50g butter
2 tablespoons vegetable oil

For garlic butter:
115g butter
pinch of finely chopped garlic
2 tablespoons fresh parsley,
    chopped
1 lemon

Wash scallops in cold water and dry them. Season with salt and pepper, then dip and roll lightly in flour. Melt butter and oil over moderate heat in frying pan. When foam subsides, sauté scallops, shaking the pan so scallops become buttered and lightly browned. Place scallops into heated dish, individual serving bowls or scallop shells. Make garlic butter as follows: Clarify butter, melting it slowly in small saucepan and skimming off foam. Pour clear butter into frying pan, discarding milk solids and heat butter until it sizzles, do not brown. Remove from heat and quickly stir in garlic. Pour garlic butter over scallops and serve at once. Garnish with chopped parsley and lemon wedges. Serves 4-6.

CRAB MEAT COCKTAIL

2 tablespoons tomato paste
2 tablespoons olive oil
2 tablespoons sweetened cream
pinch of salt and pepper
pinch of paprika
½ cup mayonnaise
2 teaspoons tomato sauce
1 teaspoon sugar
½ cup brandy
2 tablespoons dill leaves, minced
wine vinegar to thin to taste
400-500g boiled lobster or crab
    meat
mushroom heads
asparagus tips
pineapple cubes
lettuce

Blend tomato paste with oil, cream, salt, pepper and paprika and add mayonnaise. Beating with a whisk, blend in the tomato sauce, sugar, brandy and dill leaves (the flavour should be slightly alcoholic). Thin with vinegar to taste. Pour this sauce over lobster or crab meat. Blend in boiled sliced mushroom heads, asparagus tips and pineapple cubes. Serve in cocktail glasses lined with shredded lettuce. Serves 4-6.

SOUPS

BOUILLABAISSE

8 whole raw crayfish
4 onions
3 celery stalks
2 teaspoons chicken stock extract
3 carrots, finely sliced
¼ teaspoon oregano
2 teaspoons garlic salt
black pepper
8 tomatoes
2 bottles dry white wine
1 cup olive oil
3 cloves garlic, pressed
500ml fish stock
3 teaspoons parsley, chopped
pinch of powdered saffron
2-3 teaspoons Pernod
10 cooked mussels
14 cooked and shelled shrimps
250g snapper
16 slices toast

Boil whole crayfish with onions, celery, chicken stock, carrots, oregano, garlic salt and pepper to taste, in enough water to just cover crayfish. Cook for about 30 minutes. Remove crayfish and cut off tails. Cut crayfish bodies in halves lengthways. To liquid which is left add tomatoes, wine, olive oil, garlic, strong fish stock, parsley and saffron. Boil very hard for at least 10 minutes (to break up olive oil) then reduce heat and simmer to reduce liquid by one third. Add Pernod and take off heat. Cook mussels, shrimps, crayfish tails and snapper in sauce until hot. Place crayfish halves in centre of serving dish and pour bouillabaisse around crayfish head. Set toast into soup on side of serving dish and serve immediately. Serves 8.

SHRIMP SOUP

500g white fish
4 strips salt pork
6 cups water
250g shrimps
1 teaspoon butter
salt and pepper
thyme
grated lime peel
2 cloves
flour
squeeze of lime or lemon juice

Make fish stock by boiling fish and pork in water until reduced to two-thirds. Discard pork. Separate flesh of shrimps, pound heads, tails and skins finely. Remove fish and add ground shrimp heads and shrimp flesh to stock. Add butter, seasonings and cloves and boil 10 minutes. Remove shrimps, cut into small pieces and place in soup tureen. Boil rest of ingredients 30 minutes more. Thicken with flour and pour over shrimps with squeeze of lime or lemon juice. Serves 4-6.

OYSTER SOUP

3 tablespoons melted butter
12 oysters
3 tablespoons flour
600ml milk
300ml fish stock
salt and pepper
parsley, chopped

Melt butter over medium heat, add oysters and brown very lightly. Add flour and blend thoroughly. Combine milk and stock and add to pan one third at a time, stirring constantly. Bring to boil. Remove oysters from liquid and cut off beards. Cut fleshy part of oysters in halves, and return to soup. Replace but do not boil. Season to taste, serve sprinkled with finely chopped parsley. Serves 4.

SCOTCH MUTTON BROTH

800-900g mutton scrag
pinch of salt
3 cups pearl barley
1 large carrot
½ savoy cabbage
½ bunch celery with leaves
1 parsley root
½ cup green peas
½ cup turnips, chopped
½ cup potatoes, chopped
1 bunch parsley
lovage leaves
salt and pepper

Cut meat into bite-sized pieces (a few smallish bones may be allowed to remain). Place in a pot with plenty of water and salt and bring to the boil. Simmer. Add barley after 45 minutes and simmer for a further 10 minutes, adding more water if necessary. Add chopped vegetables, parsley in whole sprigs and lovage. Simmer until chopped vegetables are cooked and season to taste with salt and pepper. Serves 6-8.
Note: Like all mutton broths this soup must be eaten hot otherwise the fat is unpleasantly predominant.

CLEAR OXTAIL SOUP

1 whole oxtail
4 tablespoons dripping
½ bunch of celery
2 carrots, chopped
4 onions, chopped
3 cloves, whole
1 parsley root
1 sprig of thyme
½ tablespoon mace
8 peppercorns
1 tablespoon salt
port or white wine

Chop fresh oxtail into bite-sized pieces and cook for about 15 minutes in salted water. Pour off water and dry oxtail with a cloth. Heat dripping in a saucepan and sauté meat with vegetables, spices and salt. Quickly pour over water to cover, in order to prevent the delicate ingredients from burning. Ladle scum from the surface. Continue to cook soup gently. As soon as meat falls away from bones, strain the liquid through a sieve. If it is not clear enough, run it once or twice through a kitchen cloth. Return meat bits and vegetables to soup, cooking until meat and vegetables are done. Before serving enrich flavour with a splash of port or white wine. Serves 4-6.

CHICKEN AND VERMICELLI SOUP

450g chicken, jointed
1½ teaspoons freshly ground black
    pepper
salt
150g mushrooms
2 tablespoons white wine
1 teaspoon lemon juice
2 teaspoons butter
thyme
bay leaves
parsley
1 onion, sliced vertically
28g transparent vermicelli, cooked

Bring 9 cups water to the boil, add chicken and freshly ground pepper and simmer, skimming when necessary. Add salt to taste, and continue boiling until meat bones separate easily. Stem and soak mushrooms in water for 10 minutes. Place mushrooms in a pan, sprinkle with salt and pepper and add white wine, lemon juice, butter and herbs. Cover and cook over a low heat until tender. Add the onion and mushroom liquid to chicken broth and bring to a boil. Simmer until onion is tender, return mushrooms to broth, add the vermicelli and salt to taste. Serve hot. Serves 6-8.

CHICKEN BALLS IN CONSOMMÉ

4 baby onions, finely chopped
3 dried mushrooms soaked in
    lukewarm water and finely
    chopped
ginger, peeled and chopped
600g uncooked chicken, ground
chilli powder
1 egg
1½ teaspoons salt
6 cups chicken broth
3 sprigs parsley

Add onions, mushrooms and ginger to ground chicken meat along with chilli powder, egg and salt. Mix together well with hands and mould into balls 2.5cm in diameter. Bring broth to quick boil, reduce heat and add chicken balls to simmering liquid. Remove balls when they float to surface. Do not over-boil, and remove foam as it forms. Salt broth to taste and simmer again. Add chicken balls to warm them and place entire mixture in soup bowl. Sprinkle with parsley cut into 4cm lengths. Serves 4-6.

CHICKEN NOODLE SOUP

50g uncooked chicken meat
a little hot Chinese cabbage,
    (pickled)
3-4 bamboo shoots
30g ham
1 Chinese mushroom, soaked
handful of snow-peas
1 x 12cm leek
30g round egg noodles (chuka-soba)
500ml chicken stock
¼ teaspoon salt
½ teaspoon monosodium glutamate

Shred chicken meat, Chinese cabbage, bamboo shoots, ham, soaked mushroom, snow-peas and leek. Drop noodles into boiling water and boil for 5-6 minutes. Drain, rinse and drain again then set aside. Bring chicken stock to boiling point. Separate chicken meat and add with cabbage, bamboo shoots, ham, mushroom, snow-peas and leek to stock, cook for 2 minutes. Add salt, monosodium glutamate and cooked noodles and boil for 1 minute. Remove to tureen or soup bowl and serve immediately. Serves 4.
Note: If this is not served immediately, the noodles will become soaked with soup.

COLD CREAM OF AVOCADO SOUP

1 avocado, peeled and diced
500ml chicken stock
Tabasco sauce to taste
1 teaspoon coriander, ground
1 cup cream

Blend avocado pieces with chicken stock and add Tabasco sauce and coriander. Heat in a double-boiler for a few minutes, cool completely, add cream and chill thoroughly in refrigerator. Serves 4.

CUCUMBER SOUP

1 young cucumber, peeled
salt
50g butter
4 cups very strong bouillon
½ cup chopped sorrel leaves
pinch of salt
cayenne pepper
rice flour
2 egg yolks
1 cup milk
juice of ½ lemon

Thinly slice cucumber. Salt, cover and set aside for 2 hours. Later, pour off cucumber juice. Melt butter in a saucepan; add cucumber slices and pour on the bouillon. Cook for 15 minutes adding more bouillon if necessary. Add sorrel leaves, salt and cayenne pepper and thicken with a little rice flour. Remove from heat. Stir egg yolks into milk and stir this mixture into the soup. Add lemon juice and serve. Serves 4-6.

Beef and Green Pepper and Chicken Noodle Soup

BROCCOLI SOUP

½ rasher of bacon, sliced into squares
25g butter
1 small onion, finely chopped
500g broccoli, finely chopped
1l stock
25g flour
¼l cream
salt and pepper
toast cut in small triangles

Place chopped bacon in boiling water for one minute and strain. Melt butter in a saucepan and add onion, bacon, broccoli. Simmer for a few minutes stirring constantly. Add mixture to stock and simmer until broccoli is cooked. Remove broccoli from stock. Set aside best pieces and sieve the rest. Return to stock, with flour and cream. Continue stirring, season with salt and pepper, add broccoli pieces. Serve with triangular-cut toast. Serves 4-6.

CUCUMBER CREAM SOUP SWISS STYLE

500ml cream
500ml buttermilk
½ cucumber
juice of 1 lemon
½ teaspoon salt
½ teaspoon sugar
pinch cayenne pepper
1 tablespoon dill, chopped
1 tablespoon butter
1 clove garlic
4 slices white bread

Mix cream and buttermilk. Dice seeded and peeled cucumber, add to cream and buttermilk and season with lemon juice, salt, sugar, pepper and dill. Make garlic butter and spread on slices of toasted bread, serve with cold soup. Serves 4-6.

COLD FRESH HERB SOUP

3 tablespoons vegetable oil
½ cup fresh spinach
¼ head lettuce
1 tablespoon fresh mint
1 tablespoon fresh dill
½ tablespoon parsley, chopped
750ml water or beef stock
250g potatoes
1 clove garlic
1-2 tablespoons lemon juice
1 teaspoon salt
pinch of pepper
1 cup plain yoghurt
croutons

Heat oil in pan and add spinach, lettuce, mint, dill and parsley (all cut into fine slices). Pour water or stock on immediately, then add potatoes, which have been peeled and sliced very finely and simmer until cooked. Add finely chopped garlic and season well with lemon juice, salt and pepper. Chill well before serving. Pour yoghurt into soup and serve with croutons. Serves 4-6.

Minestrone Soup and Côte de Porc Bologna

GAZPACHO

1¼ cups tomato juice
½ cup iced water
6 tablespoons olive oil
2-3 tablespoons lemon juice
½ clove garlic
1kg ripe tomatoes, coarsley
  chopped
1 cucumber, coarsely chopped
½ onion, chopped
salt and freshly ground black
  pepper
cayenne pepper
½ green pepper, diced
4 slices white bread, diced and
  sautéed until crisp and golden
  in butter and olive oil
1 avocado pear, peeled, stoned,
  diced and brushed with lemon
  juice to preserve color
4 tablespoons parsley, coarsely
  chopped

Combine tomato juice, iced water, olive oil and lemon juice in a large soup tureen or serving bowl which has been rubbed with garlic. Add peeled, seeded and chopped tomatoes (be sure to add all the juice), peeled and chopped cucumber and onion, and generous amounts of salt, black pepper and cayenne to taste. Chill thoroughly. Serve soup in individual soup bowls with an ice cube in each bowl. Garnish with sprinkling of diced green pepper, fried croutons, diced avocado and chopped parsley. Serves 4.

VALASIAN VEGETABLE SOUP WITH CHEESE

2 leeks
1 small head cauliflower
2 onions
bunch parsley
1 cup celery leaves
salt
30g rice
500g long or star-shaped noodles
2 teaspoons flour
30g butter
salt and pepper
12 slices cheese

Cut leeks into fine strips, the cauliflower into flowerets and onions into paper-thin slices. Chop up parsley and celery leaves. Cook these vegetables in salted water for 30 minutes over a low heat. Add rice and noodles. Cook for 15 minutes. In a frying pan brown flour in butter. Slake thickening with water and stir into the soup. Season and pour into a tureen lined with sliced cheese. Serve with sliced white bread. Serves 4.

MALAYAN SPINACH SOUP

2 onions, sliced
4 tablespoons ham bacon
1.4kg chopped spinach, washed
1 cup water
1 tablespoon flour
salt and pepper
nutmeg
ground paprika
700ml milk
1 cup boiled ham strips
2 slices white bread, cubed

Brown onion slices with ham bacon, drain and save fat. Add washed spinach and water. Cook spinach completely (about 20 minutes). Add flour mixed with a little water and the spices. Pour milk into soup, add ham strips, bring to the boil and serve in a tureen. Serve with white bread cubes tossed in the ham bacon fat. Serves 4.
Note: Instead of spinach, you can use sorrel, making the soup very spicy and refreshing.

SWEET-SOUR CABBAGE SOUP

900g streaky beef, cubed
½ teaspoon cinnamon
¼ teaspoon cloves
1 teaspoon dried ginger
2 teaspoon coriander
½ teaspoon nutmeg
¼ teaspoon pepper
2 teaspoons sugar
5 splashes soy sauce
2 tablespoons white wine
salt
½ cup shallots
2 tablespoons butter
12 miniature onions
1 white cabbage, finely sliced
parsley, chopped

The streaky beef should be from young beef or oxen. Remove all gristle. Cook the meat with water and all the ground spices and sugar for 1 hour in a deep soup pot, over a low heat. Add soy sauce, white wine, salt, shallots browned in butter, miniature onions and white cabbage. When all ingredients are cooked, sprinkle soup with freshly chopped parsley. Serves 4-6.

MINESTRONE

225g fresh beans
2 carrots, diced
½ small cabbage, shredded
1 cup fresh peas
2 potatoes, diced
1 small stalk celery (remove leaves)
1 onion, diced
40g ham, diced
1 clove garlic (optional)
1 tablespoon lard
2 tablespoons chopped parsley
salt
pepper
2 tablespoons tomato paste or sauce (optional)
50g rice, cooked
Parmesan cheese, grated

Clean and wash vegetables. Place beans and carrots in a pot, cover with water and let simmer until half done. Add cabbage, peas, potatoes, celery and onion. Fry diced ham lightly with garlic and add ham, lard, and chopped parsley to soup. Salt and pepper to taste. If soup is too thick, add more water and let simmer for half an hour. A little tomato paste or sauce may be added to soup. Add cooked rice. Before serving sprinkle generously with grated Parmesan. Serves 4.

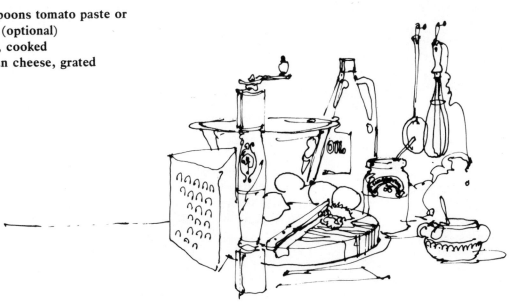

FISH

PACIFIC STYLE SEAFOOD SAUCE

2 cloves garlic, crushed
1 onion, finely chopped
4 tablespoons oil
6 fresh tomatoes or 1½ cups canned
  tomatoes
salt and pepper
½ teaspoon sugar
¼ cup lemon juice
1 cup water
500g raw or cooked shellfish,
  prawns or crayfish
2 tablespoons chopped parsley
1 teaspoon chopped fresh basil

In a pot, stir fry garlic and onion until golden. Stir in peeled and chopped tomatoes. Add salt and pepper, sugar, lemon juice and water. Cook slowly for 20 minutes. Add raw or lightly cooked shellfish, prawns or crayfish, simmer 5-10 minutes. Add parsley and if possible, basil. Serve with rice. Serves 4.

POLYNESIAN ROLLED FISH

12 fillets sole
salt and pepper
3 large bananas
oil
450g small potatoes, peeled, boiled
  and drained
¾ cup coconut, shredded
3 large carrots, scooped into small
  balls
450g green peas, shelled
2 tablespoons butter

For cocktail sauce:
tomato sauce mixed with a little
  fruit juice

Sprinkle sole fillets with salt and pepper. Peel bananas, cut into 8cm lengths and then into 6-8 longitudinal sections. Lay 3 pieces of banana at the end of each fillet and roll up in the fillet. Fasten with a toothpick. Deep fry rolled fillets in oil until golden brown. Keeping fish warm, deep fry potatoes and shredded coconut until golden. Boil carrots and green peas separately, each in salted water and drain. Soak green peas in salted water to remove wrinkles. Melt butter in pan and sauté carrots and green peas, seasoning with salt and pepper. Arrange fish, potatoes, coconut, carrots and peas on a dish and serve hot with cocktail sauce. Serves 6.

FILLETS OF SOLE IN SAKI SAUCE

2 large soles (8 fillets)
2 onions, minced
salt
½ cup candied ginger, grated
pepper
½ teaspoon sugar
220ml rice wine (saki)
1 cup onion, cubed
butter
2 eggs, beaten

Cut fillets from soles, rinse, dry and sprinkle with minced onions and salt. Mix ginger with salt and pepper and sugar into rice wine and boil with onion cubes until creamy sauce results. Lay fish fillets in a buttered baking dish, pour on sauce and brush with the eggs. Cook fillets in the oven at 150°C for 20 minutes. Serve with rice. Serves 2-4.

FILLET OF SOLE FIORDLAND

2 small shallots, chopped
120g young tender mussels, minced
150g fresh button mushrooms,
   minced
white wine
salt and pepper
400-500g trimmed and skinned fillet
   of sole
100ml fish stock (use bones of sole)
1 bay leaf
4-5 peppercorns
350ml sauce vin blanc
3-4 tablespoons hollandaise sauce
juice of ½ a lemon
butter

Sauté shallots and mushrooms in a little butter. Add half the amount of shallots and mushrooms to mussels. Moisten with a little wine and simmer until purée is quite thick. Season to taste, add lemon juice and keep warm. Poach sole in fish stock with bay leaf, remainder of shallots, peppercorns. When cooked remove sole, reduce cooking liquid and sauce vin blanc and simmer until thick and creamy. Strain and beat hollandaise sauce into mixture. Pour over sole which has been arranged on purée of mushrooms and mussels. Flash off under grill and serve. Serves 6.

PINEAPPLE FISH

500g snapper fillet
1 cup self-raising flour
pinch of salt
1 egg
1¼ cups water
pinch of monosodium glutamate
2 tablespoons brown sugar
1 tablespoon cornflour
2 tablespoons vinegar
1 tablespoon soy sauce
1 teaspoon fresh ginger, very finely
   chopped
¾ cup pineapple syrup
oil for deep frying
4 pineapple rings, chopped
toasted flaked almonds

Skin fish and cut into bite-sized pieces. Sift flour and salt together in a mixing bowl, make a well in the centre and add egg. Mix with a little of the flour using a wooden spoon. Gradually add half the water and draw in flour. Beat until batter is smooth adding the monosodium glutamate. Mix together brown sugar, cornflour, vinegar, soy sauce, ginger, pineapple syrup, salt and remaining water. Bring to the boil, stirring, and boil for 3 minutes. Dip fish pieces in batter and fry until golden brown. Drain. Add pineapple pieces to the sauce and reheat. Sprinkle fish pieces with almonds and pour over sauce. Serves 4.

SNAPPER WITH MUSHROOMS

750g snapper fillets
flour
salt
egg, beaten
breadcrumbs
100g butter
200g small mushrooms
1 onion, chopped
1 tablespoon parsley, chopped
½ tablespoon chervil, chopped
vinegar
25g butter
parsley and lemon for garnish

Dip snapper fillets in a salted flour, then beaten egg and breadcrumbs. Fry in butter until browned and cooked. While frying fish sauté onions, mushrooms etc. in a separate pan otherwise there will be a lot of burnt breadcrumbs in the onion mushroom mixture. Add more butter to pan and sauté mushrooms, onion and the chopped herbs. Add a little vinegar. Place fish fillets on a preheated dish, cover with mushroom, onion and herb mixture and garnish with parsley and lemon. Serve with mashed potatoes, buttered peas and carrots, white wine. Serves 4-6.

STUFFED SNAPPER

1 tablespoon onions, chopped
1 tablespoon chives, chopped
1 tablespoon celery, chopped
1 tablespoon ham, chopped
1 clove garlic, chopped
1 tomato, peeled and chopped
2 slices bread, soaked in milk
   and toasted
12 oysters or young mussels
1 tablespoon chip chip (or baby
   clams)
1 egg yolk
salt and pepper
a dash of Tabasco sauce
1 x 500g red snapper
3 cleaned shrimps
1 tablespoon butter
½ cup fish stock
½ cup dry white wine
4 lime wedges
1 tablespoon parsley, chopped

Sauté onions, chives, celery, ham and garlic. Add tomato and soaked, toasted bread (pressed dry) and the oysters, chip chip and egg yolk. Season to taste with salt and pepper and a dash of Tabasco sauce. Remove head and tail from fish. Clean and gut from head end – do not slit belly or back. Wash well and stuff with onion-seafood mixture. Garnish with shrimps. Place in a buttered baking dish, add fish stock and white wine until quarter of the fish is covered. Bake in the oven at 175°C for 25 minutes. Place fish on a dish and garnish with lime wedges and parsley. Serve with a white sauce. Serves 4.

FRIED FISH BAKED IN COCONUT CREAM

750g fish fillets, any kind
flour
salt and pepper
¼ cup oil
500ml coconut cream
1 onion, finely chopped

Cut fish into 4cm pieces and roll in seasoned flour. Heat oil in a pan and fry fish until browned. Place in a baking dish and pour over coconut cream flavoured with salt. Sprinkle with onion. Cover and bake at 130°C for 1 hour. Do not allow cream to boil – it will separate if it does. Serves 4.

SPICED FISH AND CUCUMBER

500g fish fillets, any kind
1 teaspoon salt
lemon juice
¼ cup flour
2 tablespoons curry powder
1 small onion, finely chopped
3 tablespoons oil
1 small cucumber, cubed or sliced
1 cup coconut cream
parsley or coriander, chopped

Cut fish into servings. Sprinkle with salt and lemon juice and leave for 15 minutes. Sift flour with salt to taste and curry powder. Stir fry onion in oil then move to one side of the pan. Coat fish in flour mixture and fry until brown on both sides. Combine fish with onion and cucumber. Pour over coconut cream. Cover pan and simmer until fish is cooked. Serve sprinkled with chopped parsley or coriander. Serves 4.

GRILLED HAPUKA (GROPER)

1-1.2kg hapuka (groper)
juice of 1 lemon
salt and pepper
olive oil
300ml sauce bearnaise

Season hapuka with lemon juice and salt and pepper. Dip in olive oil and cook on grill. Serve with sauce béarnaise. Serves 4-6.

SIMMERED FISHTAILS

2 fish tails (about 750g) of grass fish
  or fresh trout
4 tablespoons oil
15cm section of green onion
6 slices of ginger root
1 tablespoon rice wine
½ tablespoon cornflour
1 teaspoon sesame oil
½ teaspoon vinegar
4 stalks green onions or leeks,
  shredded

For sauce:
3 tablespoons soy sauce
1½ cups water
½ teaspoon monosodium glutamate
1 tablespoon sugar
¼ teaspoon black pepper

Cut each tail in half lengthways then each half into 3 sections (to make total of 12 sections). Heat pan and add oil. Stir fry onion section and ginger until fragrant, add fish tail sections (skin-side down) and fry for a few minutes until golden brown. Add rice wine and sauce mixture, cover and simmer 10 minutes until liquid has reduced by half. Mix cornflour with a little water to a smooth paste and stir into sauce. Flip fish over, add sesame oil and vinegar and lightly mix or toss the ingredients together. Turn out onto a serving dish, sprinkle with shredded green onion and serve. Serves 6.

BAKED HAPUKA (GROPER) GREAT BARRIER STYLE

3kg groper with head and tail
salt and pepper
juice of 1 lemon
¼ cup cooking oil
1 onion, chopped
½ sweet pepper, sliced
6 stewed tomatoes
½ teaspoon thyme

Rub cleaned fish with salt and pepper and lemon juice and lay on a baking dish greased with a little oil. Fry onion and pepper in hot oil. Add tomatoes and thyme and cook gently for 15 to 20 minutes, then pour mixture over the fish. Bake in 180°C oven for 25 minutes. Serve with roasted baby kumaras (sweet potatoes). Serves 6.

BRAISED CARP WITH GINGER AND SPRING ONIONS

1 carp (about 750g) trout or bream
  can be substituted
170g ginger
170g spring onions
several tablespoons butter
2 tablespoons dry sherry
1 cup fish stock
1 teaspoon salt
1 teaspoon sugar
dash of sesame oil
pinch of pepper
1 teaspoon black soy sauce
½ teaspoon cornflour
oil

Scale, gut and wash carp. Pound ginger and slice lengthways. Wash and cut spring onions into same-length pieces. Sauté ginger in butter and remove. Add carp to pan and fry for a moment. Turn fish over and sprinkle sherry over it. Add stock, salt and sugar. Turn fish mixture into earthenware pot, cover, and braise for 10 minutes. Add remaining seasonings and thicken with cornflour made into a smooth paste with a little water and oil. Serve hot with ginger and spring onion slices. Serves 4.

CANTONESE FRIED FISH

500-750g fish
2 teaspoons salt
dash of pepper
1 egg
2 tablespoons cornflour
1 cup peanut oil

Leave fish whole or cut into quarters. Rub salt and pepper all over fish and leave to stand for 15 minutes. Mix egg and 1 tablespoon cornflour together, beat well. Dip fish into egg and cornflour mixture and roll in remainder of cornflour. Heat oil to 180°C, add fish and fry until golden brown, about 5-7 minutes each side. Serve with Chinese hot sauce. Serves 4.

JAPANESE FISH CASSEROLE

700g fish fillets
salt and pepper
garlic salt
90g butter or margarine
4 tablespoons soy sauce
1 knife-tip cayenne pepper
juice of 1 lemon
4 eggs

Use a fish with firm meat for this recipe. Mix up salt and pepper and garlic salt and rub thoroughly into fish which has been cut into strips. Grease inside of baking dish with butter or margarine. Place fish in dish and bake for 10 minutes in a hot oven. During this time blend soy sauce with cayenne pepper and lemon juice; add eggs and beat with a whisk until smooth. Pour this mixture over fish and return to oven. (The eggs serve to stick the pieces of fish together.) Serve with a colourful rice casserole into which peas, red pepper, tomato strips and ham strips have been mixed. Serves 4.

MARINATED FISH

900g mild-flavoured fish steaks
½ cup olive oil
1 large onion, sliced
2 cloves garlic, peeled
½ cup green chillies, seeded and
    chopped
½ cup vinegar
¼ teaspoon ground cumin
1 teaspoon salt
juice of 1 orange
lettuce, sliced oranges, ripe olives,
    and sliced hard-boiled eggs for
    garnish

Sauté fish steaks in olive oil on both sides until lightly browned. Arrange in a shallow serving dish. In the same pan cook onion and the whole garlic cloves (threaded on a toothpick) until lightly browned. Discard garlic; add green chillis, vinegar, cumin, salt and the orange juice. Pour over fish and chill. Serve with garnishes. Serves 6.

CARP, POLISH STYLE, WITH SWEET SAUCE

¼ cup raisins
3 dried prunes
1.5-2kg carp or bream
salt and pepper
2 onions, sliced
2 carrots, sliced
1 leek, sliced
1 parsnip, sliced
½ bay leaf
3 peppercorns
fresh parsley
3 cups water
½ cup red wine
1 tablespoon vinegar or lemon juice
2 tablespoons unsalted butter
2 tablespoons sugar
2 tablespoons flour
2 cups fish stock
30g chopped almonds
1 teaspoon honey
1 sliced lemon

Soak raisins and prunes overnight. Clean and slice carp. Sprinkle each piece with salt and let stand for 1 hour. In a large saucepan place sliced onions, carrots, leek, parsnip, bay leaf, peppercorns and parsley. Cover with water, vinegar and wine, bring to the boil and simmer for 10 minutes. Add fish and cook over slow heat for 1-2 hours.

To prepare sauce, melt butter in separate saucepan adding sugar and sifted flour. Brown lightly. Slowly add strained fish stock. Mix well. Add raisins, prunes, almonds, honey, salt and pepper. Bring to the boil and simmer over a low flame for 20 minutes. Garnish fish with lemon slices and serve with sauce. Serves 6.

STURGEON BAKED IN SOUR CREAM

1.5kg sturgeon (or fresh tuna)
salt and pepper
flour
2 eggs, beaten
breadcrumbs
115g butter
chopped dill
chopped parsley
2 tablespoons bouillon
1 tablespoon flour
¼ cup sour cream

Cut fish into serving portions and sprinkle with salt and pepper. Roll slices in flour, dip in beaten egg and coat with breadcrumbs. Fry in butter until browned on both sides then place fish in baking dish. Sprinkle with dill and parsley. Add bouillon and flour to left-over butter in frying pan and stir well. Bring to the boil over low flame. Remove from fire and add sour cream. Stir thoroughly. Pour mixture over fish and bake in moderate oven for 10-15 minutes. Serves 4-6.

STEAMED HALIBUT WITH SPINACH

450g halibut or groper slices
salt
flour
2 onions, sliced
50g butter
1 cup sour cream or yoghurt
700g spinach
50g butter, cut into dabs

For butter egg sauce:
2 egg yolks
1 teaspoon lemon juice
1 pinch salt
75g melted butter

Season fish pieces and roll them in flour. Brown with onions in butter until golden then pour on sour cream or yoghurt and simmer for 20 minutes. Scald spinach leaves and, in another pan, arrange them on top of butter dabs. Cover and simmer without water, then lay fish slices on top and pour over butter-onion sauce and then the butter egg sauce prepared as follows: Stir egg yolks, lemon juice and salt in the top of a double-boiler until a creamy sauce forms. Gradually stir in the melted, lukewarm butter. Do not allow mixture to become too hot — pour over fish slices and place dish under hot grill. Allow sauce to darken slightly before serving. Serves 4-6.

BAKED FISH YUCATAN

1-1.5kg cod, hake or halibut

For tomato sauce:
1 onion, chopped
2 tablespoon olive oil
1 can peeled or 5 fresh tomatoes
¾ cup dry white wine
2 cloves
salt and freshly ground black
    pepper
1 level teaspoon cornflour
1 tablespoon water
12 green olives, pitted and cut into
    pieces
1 level teaspoon parsley, chopped
2 level teaspoons capers

To make tomato sauce, sauté chopped onion in olive oil until soft, add peeled tomatoes, wine, cloves, and salt and pepper to taste. Cover pan and simmer for 20 minutes. Blend cornflour and a little water to smooth paste and stir into tomato mixture. Simmer for 5 minutes longer, then add olives, parsley and capers.

Wash and dry fish and place in well-greased baking dish. Pour over tomato sauce and bake in a pre-heated moderate oven (190°C) for 35 minutes or until fish flakes easily with a fork. Baste occasionally. Serve hot with sauce. Serves 4-6.

FISH DUMPLINGS IN RED SAUCE

900g salt-water fish
4 onions, sliced thinly
50g butter
1 leek, in strips
2 bread rolls, soaked in water and
    squeezed dry
salt and pepper
ground paprika
2 eggs

For sauce:
30g flour
50g butter
4 tablespoons cream
pinch of salt
2 tablespoons red shrimp butter
½ cup crayfish or lobster tails,
    cooked

Skin and fillet fish and cut into pieces suitable for mincing. In a frying pan, brown onion in butter. Allow to cool then run through meat mincer with fish, leek strips and softened bread. To this mixture add salt and pepper, paprika to taste and the whole, raw eggs to form a uniform stuffing. Form into dumplings with a spoon and cook in gently boiling water until done. Remove dumplings and save water.

For the sauce, brown flour in butter and slake with cooking liquid from dumplings. Fold cream, salt and red shrimp butter into slightly thickened sauce and add crayfish pieces. Pour this sauce over dumplings, bring back to the boil and serve. Serves 4-6.

FILLET OF FISH MURAT (POMFRET)

600g potatoes, finely diced
lard
butter
6 artichoke bottoms, diced
3 x 500g soles or flounder
salt
milk
flour
clarified butter
juice of ½ lemon
3 large firm tomatoes, sliced thickly
chopped parsley

Fry potatoes until brown and crisp in lard then pour off fat and toss potatoes in butter. Cook artichoke bottoms in butter. Halve fillets of sole lengthways, dip in salted milk then in flour and fry brown and crisp in clarified butter. Toss fillets, potatoes and artichokes together, season and arrange in a deep dish. Sprinkle with lemon juice and brown butter. Fry tomato slices and place on top of fish mixture. Sprinkle with chopped parsley. Serves 6.

COD À LA DIEPPOISE

750g cod fillets (from whole cod)
½ cup white wine
100g small mushrooms
40g butter
30g flour
100g cooked mussels
100g cooked shrimps or small
  prawns
parsley, chopped

For fish stock:
heads, tails, bones and fins from
  cod
handful of parsley sprigs
1 onion
1 large carrot, sliced
½ teaspoon thyme
1 bay leaf
1 teaspoon peppercorns
slice of lemon

For fish stock, boil fish-heads, bones, tails and fins for about 20 minutes together with parsley, onion, carrot, thyme, bay leaf, peppercorns and lemon. Strain. Poach fish fillets in the stock (fish should be just covered by stock) then drain stock once more. Add white wine and mushrooms, boil until mushrooms are cooked then remove mushrooms. Melt butter in a saucepan, add flour and stir until mixture thickens. Make a sauce by adding about ¼ cup of the stock. Place cod fillets in a buttered ovenproof dish and cover with mussels, shrimps, mushrooms and the sauce. Place in a very hot oven for just a few seconds. Decorate with chopped parsley. Serve with french fries, salad and/or buttered carrots. Serves 4-6.

SALMON POT

600g salmon
1 cup dill leaves, chopped
pinch of salt
200g butter or margarine
1 cup water
juice of ½ lemon
½ cup sour cream

Cut the salmon into 100g pieces and place in a heatproof dish with dill leaves and top with salt and butter bits. Pour on water and cover the dish. Start to cook fish for a very few minutes over a low heat then remove cover so that water can steam away leaving only butter and fish juice. Stir in lemon and sour cream and heat fish through. Serves 4.

MACKERELS IN SOUR CREAM

4 mackerels (or similar fish
  e.g. mullet)
salt and pepper
450ml sour cream
4 tablespoons dill leaves, chopped
4 tablespoons cheese, grated
4 tablespoons hard roll-crumbs

Wash mackerels and remove backbones. Wash the 8 fillets obtained and drain. Season with salt and pepper and lay in a wide pan or an oval dish. Mix sour cream with dill leaves and pour over fish fillets. Sprinkle on grated cheese and hard roll-crumbs. Bake for about 25 minutes in a hot oven. Serves 4.

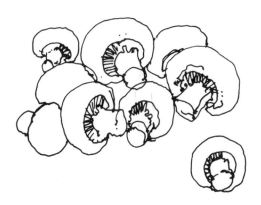

FRIED HERRING WITH ONIONS

4 green herrings
salt and pepper
2 onions, sliced
120g butter or margarine
1 egg, beaten
6 tablespoons hard roll-crumbs
230ml cream

Cut herrings open down the back and pull both fillets from the backbone at once. Skin fillets, pull out small bones, cut off the abdominal lobes. Salt and pepper fillets. Toss onions in a little butter until golden brown. Place 4 fillets skin-down on a board, distribute browned onions over them and press on matching fillets. Dip fillet pairs in beaten egg, then in hard roll-crumbs and fry in butter. (If butter becomes too hot and the bread-crumbs darken too much the fillets can finish cooking in the oven.) Pour cream over cooked herrings and warm them up once more. Serves 2-4.

BRUNSWICK CREAMED HERRING

10 fat salted herrings
450ml sour cream
1 large pickled cucumber, sliced
2 firm, slightly acid apples, sliced
2 onions, sliced
2 tablespoons chives, chopped

For marinade:
1 tablespoon vinegar
1 tablespoon water
1 tablespoon sugar

Soak salted herrings for at least 24 hours in cold water, changing the water often. Remove fillets and all bones from herrings. Prepare marinade from vinegar, water and sugar and stand fillets in it for several hours. Drain fillets and place in a serving bowl. Pour on sour cream and add slices of cucumber, apple and onion. Sprinkle with chives. Serves 4-5.

BAKED CANADIAN TROUT WITH BACON

50g butter
250g lean sliced ham bacon
2kg salmon or rainbow trout
salt and pepper
230ml sour cream

Line a buttered baking dish with most of the sliced ham bacon. Clean out and wash trout and lightly rub inside with salt and pepper. Place in baking dish and cover with remaining bacon slices. Cover dish and simmer fish for about 30 minutes at 200°C. Remove lid and brown bacon slices. Pour on sour cream and serve in the baking dish. Serves 4.

FILLETS OF TROUT 'BEAU RIVAGE'

2 large trout
60g butter or margarine
1 cup small shallots, cubed
salt
ground paprika
pepper
juice of 1 lemon
½ cup of mushrooms, chopped
2 tomatoes, sliced
2 tablespoons parsley, chopped
1 cup white wine
1 cup sour cream

Clean out trout and remove fillets, but without removing skin. Grease a flat heatproof dish and spread shallot cubes in it. Sprinkle with salt and ground paprika. Wash fillets, dry off with a cloth and season with salt and pepper and lemon juice. Arrange fillets on top of shallots and cover with mushrooms, tomatoes and parsley. Pour on the wine and cover with grease-proof paper. Cook in a moderate oven for 25 minutes, then remove dish from oven and pour juice into saucepan. Add sour cream to the saucepan and reduce slightly then pour mixture back over fillets. Serve in the baking dish. Accompany with buttered potatoes and lettuce salad. Serves 2.

TROUT TAUPO

30g butter
½ teaspoon chives, finely chopped
pinch of thyme and marjoram
½ teaspoon dill, finely chopped
1 teaspoon shallots, chopped
700-800g trout fillets
150ml white wine
350ml fish stock
50g beurre manié
lemon juice
100ml cream
1 teaspoon chopped parsley

Butter casserole dish and place in chives, thyme, marjoram, dill and shallots. Lay fillets of trout on top and pour over white wine and fish stock. Cover with greaseproof paper and poach in oven. Remove fillets and keep warm. Reduce cooking liquid in casserole, lightly bind with beurre manié. Bring to boil, add lemon juice and then cream. Pour over fillets, sprinkle with chopped parsley and serve. Serves 6.

TROUT SUPREME

1 medium size whole trout
1 cup sherry
1 cup milk
salt and pepper

For stuffing:
1 cup breadcrumbs
½ teaspoon salt
pepper
½ small onion
1 tablespoon parsley, chopped
pinch of mixed herbs
2 tablespoons butter, melted
2 tablespoons hot water

Wash and dry trout and place in casserole dish. Pour sherry over and leave overnight then remove, retaining marinade. Mix stuffing ingredients and pack into fish. Add milk to sherry, season, place trout back in liquid and bake in a moderate oven, allowing 10 minutes per 500g. Serves 1.

LOBSTER WITH BRANDY SAUCE

1 x 1.5kg cooked lobster
3 tablespoons butter
2 teaspoons olive oil
½ teaspoon salt
¼ teaspoon freshly ground black
   pepper
¼ teaspoon cayenne pepper
¾ cup brandy
2 teaspoons cornflour mixed with
   2 tablespoons water

Split lobster shell, crack claws and remove grey sac. Remove lobster meat from shell, cut into small pieces and set aside. Wipe shell halves clean and place them, with claws, in a heat-proof dish. Set dish aside. In a medium sized frying pan, melt butter with oil over moderate heat. When foam subsides, add lobster meat, salt and pepper and cayenne and fry, stirring occasionally, for 3 to 4 minutes, or until lobster meat is lightly browned.

In a small saucepan, heat brandy over low heat until it is hot but not boiling. Remove pan from heat and carefully pour brandy over lobster meat. Ignite and leave until flames have completely died down. With a slotted spoon remove lobster meat from pan and place into reserved shell halves. Return pan to moderate heat and bring back liquid to boil. Reduce heat to low and stir in cornflour mixture a little at a time, beating constantly until ingredients are blended and sauce has thickened. Remove pan from heat and pour sauce over the lobster meat. Place baking dish under the grill and grill for about 5 minutes or until the lobster is golden brown. Remove and serve at once. Serves 2.

LOBSTER AMERICAN

2 lobsters
salt
1½ cups olive oil
100g shallots, chopped
1 clove garlic, crushed
1 carrot, chopped
½ teaspoon each thyme and
  tarragon
cayenne pepper
½ cup brandy
1 small can tomato sauce
½ cup dry white wine

Remove and crack open claws from lobsters. Remove tail sections from lobsters and divide into 3 or 4 slices. Halve lobsters lengthways and discard veins and sacs. Remove livers and corals and set aside. Rub in salt on all places where lobster was cut open. Heat oil in a heavy pan, add shallots, garlic, carrot, thyme and tarragon and cook, stirring, for about 2 minutes. Add lobster and sprinkle with a little cayenne pepper. Pour in brandy and flame. Add tomato sauce, cover and simmer until shells are red and lobster meat is tender. Cool slightly and remove lobster meat from shells. Strain wine and add livers and corals. Cook, stirring constantly, for several minutes or until thickened. Add white wine and lobster meat and reheat to serving temperature. Serves 4.

CANADIAN STUFFED LOBSTER

250g mushrooms
2 tablespoons butter
1 tablespoon flour
salt and pepper
1 cup cream
3 tablespoons sherry
2 x 1kg boiled lobsters
2 tablespoons parsley, chopped

Wash mushrooms and cut into small, thin strips. Simmer gently in hot butter until brown. Sift flour into pan, add salt and pepper and stir until smooth. Add cream and simmer for another 5 minutes, stirring frequently. Remove from heat and add sherry. Mix well. Cut boiled lobsters along centre and remove meat. Break off claws, extract meat. Cut meat into pieces, mix with mushroom sauce and refill shells. Grill lobster for several minutes before serving. Garnish with chopped parsley and serve. Serves 4.

BRAISED PRAWNS WITH TOMATO

16 prawns
salt and pepper
salad oil
2 cloves garlic, crushed
400g tomatoes
160ml white wine
2 teaspoons paprika, powdered
⅔ teaspoon chilli powder
180g carrots, quartered and cut into
  5cm lengths
680g green peas, shelled

Shell and clean prawns leaving heads and tails intact. Sprinkle with salt and pepper. Heat 3 tablespoons salad oil in thick pot and sauté garlic over high heat. Lower heat and cook prawns until colour changes. Add tomatoes and continue cooking until they lose their shape. Add wine and season with salt (about 1⅓ teaspoons), pepper, paprika and chilli powder. Cover, cook over a low heat for 15 minutes and place on a serving dish, keep warm. Boil carrots until tender and drain. Boil peas in salted water. Drain. Heat salad oil in pan and sauté carrots and peas, seasoning with salt and pepper. Serve together with prawns. Serves 4.

SHRIMP PIES

For crust:
4 cups flour
1 teaspoon baking powder
3 egg yolks
230g butter
salt
1 egg yolk

For filling:
615g shrimps
4 tablespoons oil
1 large green pepper, diced
1 large onion, sliced
**milk from 1 fresh coconut or one
    cup ready made coconut milk**
3 tablespoons cheese, grated
2 egg yolks

Sift flour and baking powder onto a board. Place egg yolks, softened butter and salt into centre of the flour and mix well by hand until dough does not stick to hands. Roll and divide dough into 12 small circles, 6 large ones for base, 6 small ones for lids. Line cup-cake forms with dough. Prepare filling by frying shrimps in oil, together with the pepper and onion, until slightly brown. Add coconut milk, cheese and egg yolks. Allow to boil until mixture forms a thick cream. Spoon filling into cup-cakes and cover with another circle of dough. Press edges together carefully (dough on top should not overlap the forms). Brush pastry tops with egg yolk and bake in moderate oven for 12-15 minutes. Serves 6.

SHRIMP CROQUETTES

500g shrimps
**2 tablespoons parsley, finely
    chopped**
½ teaspoon salt
dash of pepper
3 tablespoons flour
2 tablespoons butter
½ cup milk
flour
1 egg, beaten
breadcrumbs
butter for frying

Boil shrimps in a small amount of water. Remove shrimps and cut into small pieces. Cool and save ½ cup of the water. Mix shrimps with parsley, salt and pepper. Make a smooth, thick sauce of flour, butter, milk and the ½ cup of shrimp stock. Add pinch of salt. Blend shrimps with sauce and form croquettes. Roll in flour, dip into the beaten egg and coat with breadcrumbs. Fry in deep fat until golden brown. Serves 2.

CURRIED SHRIMPS SUVA STYLE

1 onion, sliced
4 tablespoons butter
1 banana, diced
1 apple, diced
curry powder to taste
½ cup mango chutney
½ cup flour
4 cups fish stock
1 tablespoon salt
pepper to taste
juice of ½ lime
1 teaspoon Worcestershire sauce
2 tablespoons brandy
1.25kg raw shrimps, peeled
6½ bananas, crumbed for garnish

Sauté onion in half the butter together with diced banana and apple. Add curry, mango chutney and flour. Keep on low heat and stir constantly. Cook until flour browns lightly. Add fish stock, salt, pepper, lime and Worcestershire sauce and stir in the rest of the butter and brandy. Strain sauce onto shrimps and cook for another 5-10 minutes. Serve in a ring of rice and garnish with crumbed, deep-fried bananas. Serves 4-6.

SHRIMPS NEW ORLEANS STYLE

450g shrimps
5 shallots
2 tablespoons parsley, chopped
1 parsley root
2 cloves garlic
salt and pepper
2 tablespoons sweet pepper strips
1 bay leaf
½ cup oil
5 shallots
juice of 1 lemon
2 tablespoons tomato sauce
1 tablespoon grated fresh
   horseradish
2 teaspoons mustard paste
2 teaspoons paprika
cayenne pepper
1 clove garlic
1 cup mayonnaise
lettuce

Place shrimps in a flat, heat-proof baking dish along with 5 shallots, chopped parsley, parsley root, garlic, salt and pepper, sweet pepper strips and bay leaf. Dribble on the oil and cover with grease-proof paper. Cook shrimps until done (about 15 minutes) in a moderate oven. Remove shrimps and cool the rest of the contents. Blend these ingredients with another 5 shallots, the lemon juice, tomato sauce, horseradish, mustard, ground paprika, cayenne pepper and garlic into a fine purée. Stir in the mayonnaise and pour over the shrimps arranged on a bed of lettuce. Serve with toast and butter. Serves 2-4.

PRAWNS CALYPSO

24 peeled and de-veined raw king
   prawns
½ cup melted butter
½ teaspoon fresh garlic, chopped
turmeric
oregano
¼ cup brandy
2 onions, cut into matchsticks
3 red and green peppers, cut into
   matchsticks
2 tomatoes, peeled and diced
salt and white pepper

Sauté prawns in butter on a high heat. Add garlic and a dash of turmeric and oregano. Flame with brandy. When flame burns off, add onions, peppers and tomatoes. Season with salt and pepper to taste. Cover casserole and let simmer for several more minutes. Serve with steamed rice. Serves 4-6.

PRAWNS IN COCONUT MILK

1 tablespoon ghee or oil
2 onions, thinly sliced
2 cloves garlic, crushed
1 teaspoon fresh ginger, finely
   grated
2 fresh red or green chillies, slit and
   seeded
1 teaspoon ground turmeric
2 cups coconut milk
1 teaspoon salt
750g large raw prawns, washed and
   shelled
lemon juice to taste

Heat ghee and fry onions, garlic and ginger until onions are soft but not browned. Add chillies and turmeric and fry 1 minute longer. Add coconut milk and salt and stir while bringing to simmering point. Simmer uncovered for 10 minutes, then add prawns and cook for 10-15 minutes. Remove from heat and add lemon juice to taste. Serves 4.

The Opera House, Sydney

POULTRY

BUTTERED CHICKEN WITH WINE AND GRAPES

3 spring chickens
140g unsalted butter
salt and pepper
½ cup strained chicken stock
1 cup white wine
1 cup seedless white grapes

Cut each chicken in half lengthways. Heat butter in a large deep frying pan and fry chicken pieces on both sides until half-cooked. Add salt and pepper, chicken stock and wine. Cover pan and cook chickens gently until tender. Five minutes before serving add grapes. Serves 4-6.

CHICKEN STEW

2 young, or 4 baby chickens
salt
4 wide, thin slices of bacon
50g butter
2 cups bouillon
450g mussels
50g butter
1 tablespoon flour
4 cups bouillon
juice of ½ a lemon
4 tablespoons sour cream
½ cup peas
½ cup mushrooms
½ cup crayfish tails
½ cup asparagus tips

Clean young chickens, salt insides and wrap in bacon strips. Arrange side by side in hot butter in a stewing pot and pour on 2 cups of bouillon. Simmer until done, over a moderate heat. In the meantime, boil mussels for 5 minutes in salted water. Remove from shells. Next, make a light flour thickening using butter, flour and bouillon. Season to taste with lemon juice and sour cream. Add mussels, peas, mushrooms, crayfish tails and asparagus tips and bring once more to the boil. Pour this sauce with its contents over the whole chickens and serve with mashed potatoes. Serves 4-6.

CHICKEN WITH SHALLOTS AND TURNIPS

1 chicken (about 1.5kg), in pieces
125g butter
4 teaspoons oil
16 shallots (or spring onions),
    peeled
salt
freshly ground black pepper
2 bay leaves
1 teaspoon lemon juice
500g turnips, scooped into small
    balls
6 tablespoons chicken stock

Wash chicken under cold running water and dry thoroughly. Melt half the butter and oil in large frying pan over moderate heat. Brown chicken pieces on all sides and transfer to plate. Add shallots to frying pan, cook evenly until lightly coloured. Pour off nearly all the fat from pan. Return chicken to pan, season to taste with salt and pepper. Lay bay leaves on top of chicken and cover, cooking over a high heat until fat sizzles. Reduce heat at once to cook chicken slowly, basting with pan juices every 10 minutes. Meanwhile melt balance of butter in large pan then pour in lemon juice. Add turnip balls and toss until glistening. Season with salt, cover and cook on low heat until turnips are tender. Chicken should be cooked in about 30 minutes. Remove from frying pan and arrange pieces on flat, heated dish alternately with shallots and turnips. Discard bay leaves. Pour chicken stock into remaining juices in frying pan, bring quickly to the boil and boil for 3-5 minutes until sauce is reduced to about 6 tablespoons. Pour over chicken and serve at once. Serves 4-6.

Lobster with Brandy Sauce, Salad – Boston Style and Roast Sweet and Sour Turkey

BREAST OF CHICKEN FANTASY

6 chicken breasts
lemon juice
salt and pepper
6 tablespoons flour
150g butter
100g mushrooms or 15g dried
  mushrooms
2 cloves garlic
chopped parsley
50g Parmesan cheese, grated
2 eggs, beaten

Wash chicken breasts in water and lemon juice and dry with a linen cloth. Beat them with a meat pounder, leaving the little wing-bone bare. Season chicken breasts with salt and pepper, then flour lightly. Melt butter in a wide frying pan and fry chicken breasts until golden brown on both sides.

Remove chicken from frying pan when well cooked and place on a chopping board. Cut a hole in the centre of each breast with a sharp knife. Mince the meat taken out, along with mushrooms, garlic and parsley. Collect minced ingredients in a bowl, season with Parmesan cheese, salt and pepper, and bind with the beaten eggs. Make small round croquettes with this mixture and set them in the empty space in each chicken breast. Heat a little more butter in frying pan and fry stuffed chicken breasts until brown. When done, arrange on a heated, oval, serving dish, pour over the gravy in which they were cooked and decorate wing bones with paper frills. Serves 4-6.

SAUTÉED CHICKEN

3 tablespoons oil
900g spring chicken, boned and
  cut into chunks
salt and pepper
1 tablespoon unsalted roasted
  peanuts, skinned and thinly
  sliced
1 red pepper, seeded and
  shredded diagonally
3-4 stalks parsley

Heat oil and sauté chicken over a high heat until tender. Season with salt and pepper to taste. Place on a serving dish and garnish with peanuts, red pepper and parsley cut into 4cm lengths. Serves 4-6.

CHICKEN WITH ALMONDS

1 egg white
1 teaspoon sherry
salt
¼ teaspoon monosodium
  glutamate
200g uncooked chicken meat,
  diced
4 tablespoons peanut oil
500g blanched almonds
60g bamboo shoots, diced
60g water chestnuts, diced
30g cucumber, diced
pinch of sugar
¼ teaspoon monosodium
  glutamate
2 teaspoons soy sauce
1 teaspoon cornflour

Add egg white, sherry, pinch salt and ¼ teaspoon monosodium glutamate to chicken and mix well. Heat peanut oil in a pan, add almonds and fry quickly until lightly browned. Remove and drain on kitchen paper. Fry chicken in same pan and remove when cooked. Place bamboo shoots, water chestnuts and cucumber in pan and cook for 2 minutes. Add chicken, pinch of sugar, ¼ teaspoon monosodium glutamate and soy sauce. Mix cornflour with a little water and stir into mixture until mixture thickens. Add almonds, stir together well and remove to heated dish. Serves 4.

FRIED CHICKEN BITS

1 frying or very young stewing
  chicken
1 cup oil
2 cups bamboo shoots
1 cup onion, cubed
120g mushrooms, sliced
230ml chicken bouillon
1 small glass sherry
2 tablespoons soy sauce
1 tablespoon honey

Bone boiled or fried chicken and separate meat from skin. Cut meat into strips and brown lightly with oil in a frying pan, stirring well. Add bamboo shoots, onion cubes and mushroom slices. When these have been fried until golden brown, pour on a little chicken bouillon, add sherry and soy sauce and simmer for 15 minutes over a low heat until tender. Blend in the honey and serve with plain rice. Serves 4-6.

BRAISED CHICKEN WITH PEPPER

3 red peppers
oil
1 teaspoon salt
500g chicken meat, diced
30g fresh ginger, finely chopped
1 teaspoon brown sugar
2 teaspoons sherry
1 teaspoon cornflour
2 teaspoons soy sauce

Slice peppers into thin rings and fry in a little oil for a few minutes. Add about 2 tablespoons of water, bring to boil, simmer for a moment and drain. Season chicken well with salt and then fry with ginger in oil for a few minutes then add sugar and sherry. Mix cornflour with a little water to a smooth paste, combine with soy sauce and add to the pan. Add peppers and cook for a few minutes then serve. Serves 4-6.
Note: This dish is usually accompanied by rice.

CHICKEN KEBAB SOUTH PACIFIC

4 whole chicken breasts
300g walnuts or peanuts
1 cup lime juice
3 tablespoons chicken stock
  powder
2 green onions, cut up
3 small cloves garlic, mashed
1 teaspoon salt
2 cups sour cream or yoghurt

Bone uncooked chicken, cutting meat into bite-sized pieces, and set aside. Combine nuts, lime juice, chicken stock, onions, garlic and salt and blend until nuts are quite fine. Mix ½ cup of this nut mixture with yoghurt or sour cream to serve as sauce with chicken. Keep chilled. Gently coat pieces of chicken with remaining nut mixture and refrigerate for 2-3 hours. Thread coated chicken pieces onto skewers and refrigerate until you are ready to cook the meat. Serves 4.

CHICKEN NTEDZA STEW
(Peanut stew)

1 chicken
1 cup roasted peanuts
2 or 3 onions, sliced
2 or 3 bottled red chillies or a
  fresh red pepper
pinch of salt
4 hard-boiled eggs, quartered
  lengthways
oranges, sliced
dessicated coconut

Cut chicken into joints. Mince peanuts. Stew chicken gently in 2½ cups water with onions, chillies or a sliced red pepper, salt and peanuts. Cook for about 2 hours, depending on size of chicken. Stew should be a thick gravy, if necessary add more minced nuts or a little more water. Add eggs to stew just before dishing. Serve with sliced oranges and dessicated coconut. Serves 4.

CHICKEN IN PINEAPPLE

750g chicken, boiled and sliced
1 cup sliced mushrooms
3 tablespoons butter
½ cup sherry
1 tablespoon flour
2 cups chicken broth
½ cup cream
salt and pepper
lemon juice
1 tablespoon sliced roasted
   almonds
1 egg yolk
1 cup cream, whipped
2 whole pineapples
puff pastry for fleuron garnish

Sauté sliced chicken and mushrooms in a little of the butter. Add sherry and simmer until half of the sherry has evaporated. Blend the rest of the butter with flour and mix with chicken broth. Simmer for 15 minutes then add to chicken and mushrooms along with ½ cup of the cream. Mix well without mashing chicken and simmer for a few minutes. Season to taste with salt, pepper and lemon juice and add slivered almonds. Blend carefully with egg yolk and whipped cream. Cut pineapples in half lengthways. Scoop out fruit. Heat pineapple shell in a 150°C oven until hot then fill with chicken mixture garnish and glaze. Serves 4.

Fleuron garnish:
Roll out pastry to 3mm thickness. With wrinkle cut pastry cutters, cut out crescent moon shapes. Bake in oven at 200°C until golden brown. Place around pineapple to decorate and serve with each portion.
Note: You can use the pineapple meat for dessert.

LEMON CHICKEN

½ lemon
1 teaspoon dried mandarin-orange
   peel
1 slice ginger
1 large clove garlic, minced
1 teaspoon light soy sauce
1 teaspoon salt
1 tablespoon sugar
¼ to ½ teaspoon cinnamon,
   ground
2 teaspoons cornflour
2 tablespoons water
2 chickens (1-1.5kg each)

Slice lemon thinly, mince mandarin-orange peel. Mix together thoroughly, lemon, orange peel, ginger, garlic, soy sauce, salt, sugar and ground cinnamon. Mix cornflour and water and set aside. Place chicken in deep steaming bowl and spread mixed spice mixture over surface of chicken. Place bowl in steaming utensil, cover and steam 15 minutes. Uncover, turn chicken over, cover again and steam 15 to 20 minutes more. Remove chicken to serving dish and reserve juices. Bring juices to boil in small pot and add cornflour with water, stirring until sauce thickens. Pour sauce over chicken and serve. Serves 6-8.

SPRING CHICKEN IN COCONUT MILK

1 teaspoon cloves, powdered
3 tablespoons caraway seeds
15g fresh ginger, grated
1 tablespoon cardamom
3 tablespoons coriander
3 tablespoons poppy seeds
6 cloves garlic, grated
2 x 400g spring chickens, cleaned
4 tablespoons coconut oil
1⅓ cups water
2 large red onions, chopped
2-3 sprigs parsley
7 cups coconut milk
1 tablespoon salt

Mix together cloves, caraway seeds, ginger, cardamom, coriander, poppy seeds and garlic. Cut necks off chickens and remove tendons from legs. Cut chicken into four parts, retaining bones. Make incisions with sharp knife where meat is thick or where heat will not penetrate easily. Heat a thick pot and pour in the coconut oil, then add chopped onion. Sauté over a medium heat until slightly brown. Add spices – garlic mixture, 1⅓ cups water and simmer for 20 minutes. When sauce thickens, put in quartered parts of chicken along with sprigs of parsley. After cooking for about 5 minutes, add coconut milk. Then add salt and stir well. Place lid over pot and cook, stirring occasionally, until chicken meat separates easily from bones. Pour broth into bowl and serve with chicken. Serves 4-6.
Note: If coconut milk not available make an infusion of 1 cup of dessicated coconut to 7 cups of water. Strain and use.

EMPRESS CHICKEN

8 chicken legs
8 chicken thighs
375g prosciutto ham
¼ cup sherry
¼ cup soy sauce
1 teaspoon salt
¼ teaspoon pepper
½ teaspoon monosodium
    glutamate
2 tablespoons oil
cornflour
oil for deep frying

For sauce:
12 Chinese dried black
    mushrooms
2 tablespoons oil
¼ cup onions, chopped
1 tablespoon ginger root, chopped
3 cups chicken stock
½ teaspoon salt
30ml sherry
30ml soy sauce
3 tablespoons cornflour mixed
    with ½ cup cold water

Wash chicken legs and thighs and bone carefully, leaving skin intact. Chop prosciutto ham very fine and fill cavity of each leg and thigh. Mix sherry, soy sauce, seasonings and oil in a bowl and marinate chicken 10 to 15 minutes. Roll pieces in cornflour, rubbing it in to make a good coating, and fry in deep fat until golden brown. Keep warm in oven while you make sauce.
Wash and soak mushrooms in warm water for 15 to 20 minutes. When spongy, squeeze out water and cut into strips 5mm wide. Heat pan and add oil; sauté onions and chopped ginger together. Add mushrooms and stir fry a few seconds, then add chicken stock, salt, sherry and soy, and bring to a boil. Thicken with cornflour mixture, then add fried chicken pieces and heat through. Serve with steamed rice. Serves 6-8.

CHICKEN HARI KEBAB

1kg chicken
salt to taste
2 teaspoons vinegar
1 teaspoon turmeric powder
1 teaspoon sugar
230g cauliflower, chopped
230g potatoes, chopped
230g carrots, chopped
ghee or oil
5 cloves garlic, chopped
3 large onions, sliced
1 tablespoon chilli powder
1 teaspoon turmeric powder
2 tablespoons ginger juice
2 cups white flour
¼ cup margarine
3 eggs, beaten
1 small can thick cream
few small onions
2 tablespoons green peas
few tomatoes, sliced
few fresh chillies

Cut chicken into pieces – wash and rub with salt, vinegar, 1 teaspoon turmeric powder, sugar. Set aside for 3 hours. Fry cauliflower, potatoes and carrots with salt and ghee for a few minutes and remove. Reheat ghee, add garlic and sliced onions and fry, then add chicken, chilli powder, turmeric powder and ginger juice. Fry until liquid has boiled off then add water to cover. Mix the flour with margarine and rub well, add 1 beaten egg and a little water then knead well and make a hard dough. Set aside for 2-3 hours. When chicken is three-quarters cooked add cauliflower, potatoes and carrots and cover again. Beat the remaining 2 eggs with the cream and set aside. When chicken and vegetables are cooked, add small onions and beaten cream. Mix well and remove from heat. Place chicken mixture into a deep pudding bowl then add peas, tomatoes and fresh chillies. Roll out dough with a little ghee and cover top of pudding bowl. Close edges well, place in moderate oven and bake until pudding rises and is slightly brown. Remove and serve. Serves 4-6.

CHICKEN IN CRISP NOODLE BASKET

250g dried Chinese noodles
700g chicken meat, sliced into
    bite-sized pieces and salted
oil for frying
4 green peppers, seeded, sliced
    lengthways into 8 sections
2 sweet red peppers, seeded,
    sliced lengthways into 8 sections
4 tablespoons oil
1½ tablespoons soy sauce
1½ tablespoons wine
⅔ teaspoon salt
2 teaspoons sugar
⅔ cup chicken stock
1 tablespoon cornflour mixed with
    2 tablespoons water

Boil noodles in salt water and drain. Slice chicken into bite-sized pieces and salt.
Two metal 25cm sieves are necessary to prepare the 'basket'. Heat oil to 140°C and place one of the sieves in the oil. When it is thoroughly hot spread noodles over entire surface and press the other sieve down over noodles. Deep fry until noodles are crisp and brown then remove noodle 'basket' carefully so that it retains its shape. Sauté chicken in 2 tablespoons oil over a high heat until golden. Remove from heat. Sauté green and red peppers in another 2 tablespoons oil over a high heat, add sautéed chicken, soy sauce, wine, sugar, and soup stock and bring to the boil. Thicken with mixture of cornflour and water. Lay noodle-basket on plate and in basket arrange sautéed peppers and chicken. This dish can be served on a bed of crisp noodles. Serves 6-8.

CHICKEN GIBLETS AND CUCUMBER

600-700g chicken giblets
2 tablespoons wine
leek greens
1 piece ginger, crushed
oil
1 egg, beaten lightly with pinch of
    salt
600g cucumber, shredded in 3cm
    lengths
1 piece ginger, skinned and
    shredded

For sauce:
3 tablespoons soy sauce
2 tablespoons vinegar
1 teaspoon sugar
1 teaspoon sesame oil

Clean and trim giblet and soak in water for 15 minutes. Place in boiling water along with wine, leek leaves and ginger and boil until giblets are tender. Drain. Shred giblets after they have cooled. Warm pan, coat thinly with oil, pour in egg and fry over a low heat. When cooked, shred in 3cm lengths. Mix giblets with cucumber and ginger, arrange on a serving dish and garnish with shredded egg. Mix ingredients for sauce and pour over giblets and cucumber just before serving. Serves 6-8.

CHICKEN WITH BARBECUED OYSTERS

500g chicken breast meat, diced
2 teaspoons cornflour
1 teaspoon five-spice powder
1 teaspoon salt
oil for frying
1 clove garlic, crushed
½ cup chicken stock
2 teaspoons extra cornflour
2 tablespoons cold water
24 barbecued oysters

Remove skin and bones from chicken meat. Toss in a mixture of cornflour, five-spice and salt. Heat 2 tablespoons oil in a wok and stir fry garlic a few seconds. Add chicken pieces and stir fry over high heat for 2-3 minutes or until chicken starts to colour. Push chicken to side of wok, add stock, then stir in extra cornflour mixed with cold water. Stir over medium heat until mixture boils and thickens, then add oysters and toss all together until heated through. Serves 6.

MEXICAN CHICKEN

4 large chicken pieces
45-60g flour
salt and pepper
large pinch of garlic powder
2 onions, sliced
2 tomatoes, chopped
75g butter
60ml white wine
¾ cup chicken stock
60-85g raisins
60g pimento-stuffed olives
bouquet garni (parsley, bay leaf
    and thyme)
½ teaspoon salt
¼ teaspoon pepper
¼ teaspoon cinnamon
3 tablespoons slivered almonds,
    browned in butter

Preheat oven to 190°C. Roll chicken pieces in flour seasoned with salt, garlic powder and pepper. Toss onions in the same flour, and set aside. Melt butter and when foaming fry chicken pieces until golden brown, about 7-10 minutes. Remove; keep warm in an ovenproof casserole. Add onions and tomatoes to butter and cook for 4-5 minutes. Add wine, stock, raisins, olives, herbs and seasoning. Bring to boil, remove bouquet garni, and pour over chicken pieces. Cook in oven for 35 minutes or until chicken is tender. Sprinkle chicken with cinnamon and stir into sauce. Sprinkle over browned almonds and serve at once with plain boiled rice. Serves 4.

CHICKEN WITH GINGER – (Kai Phat Khing)

¾ cup chopped scallions, both
    green and white
2 cloves garlic, crushed
2 tablespoons salad oil
¼ cup fresh minced or crystallised
    ginger
1½ tablespoons soy sauce
1½ tablespoons vinegar
1½ tablespoons sugar
1 x 1.75kg chicken, boned
    and diced
¼ teaspoon salt
¼ teaspoon pepper
½ cup chicken stock
1 cup mushrooms, sliced
parsley

Sauté scallions and garlic in oil. Add ginger, soy sauce, vinegar and sugar and stir until dissolved. Add chicken and stir fry for 2-3 minutes. Add salt, pepper and stock. Bring to a boil then cover and simmer over a low heat until chicken is done, about 30 minutes. Add mushrooms and cook for 5 minutes longer. Garnish with parsley and serve with boiled rice. Serves 4-6.

HOT AND SPICY CHICKEN

1kg chicken meat
2 tablespoons shredded ginger
1 tablespoon sherry
1 tablespoon light soy sauce
½ cup chicken broth
2 tablespoons wine vinegar
1 tablespoon sugar
sesame oil
salt
4 tablespoons oil
1 scallion or a spring onion, sliced
2 red hot peppers, sliced
cornflour

Cut chicken into bite-sized pieces and marinate in ginger, sherry and soy sauce. Mix chicken broth with wine vinegar, sugar, sesame oil, salt and leave to stand. Heat a pan, add the 4 tablespoons oil and stir fry scallion and peppers for a few minutes. Add chicken and marinade and stir fry for a few more minutes. Pour in chicken broth mixture and thicken with cornflour mixed with a little water to a smooth consistency. Serve hot on a bed of rice. Serves 4-6.

PAELLA VALENCIANA

12 shrimps
12 mussels
2 small frying chickens, each
    jointed into 8 pieces
225g lean pork
2 large spanish onions, chopped
    fine
⅓ cup olive oil
1 tomato, skinned and crushed
1 clove garlic, crushed
1½ cups rice
125g eel (optional)
handful fresh lima beans
handful sweet peas
2 bottoms of artichokes cut in
    quarters
2 sweet red peppers
3 cups seafood liquid
½ bay leaf
salt and pepper
¼ teaspoon saffron

Shell and cook shrimps and mussels. Save 3 cups of liquid. Paella is cooked in a heavy iron pot with a round bottom, called paellera. Any heavy pot with a tight cover may be substituted. Brown chicken, pork and onions in a third of a cup of olive oil, add tomato and garlic. Mix well. Add rice and fry for 2 or 3 minutes. Add seafood and raw eel, beans, peas, artichokes, red peppers. Pour the 3 cups of seafood liquid over mixture and bring to the boil. Add bay leaf, salt, pepper and saffron. Cook over a brisk heat for 5 minutes, mixing frequently. Lower heat, cover pot, and simmer gently for about 15-18 minutes or until rice absorbs the liquid and is quite dry. If baked, let cook in oven for 45 minutes. Serve with additional red peppers on top. Serves 6.

CHICKEN CURRY

2 x 2kg stewing chickens
1 teaspoon salt
⅛ teaspoon dry red pepper
2 cups yoghurt
4 onions, sliced finely
4 cloves garlic, minced
2.5cm piece of green ginger,
    minced
1 cup butter or fat
2 teaspoons coriander powder
1 teaspoon turmeric powder
1 teaspoon ground cumin seeds
½ teaspoon chilli powder
½ teaspoon powdered mustard
1 teaspoon cinnamon
1 teaspoon crushed cloves
2 tomatoes, chopped
1 bouillon cube
3 cups boiling water
juice of 1 lime or lemon

Clean and cut chicken into small sections, sprinkle with salt and red pepper. Cover with yoghurt and let stand for 30 minutes. Brown onions, garlic, and ginger in butter, add other spices and mix well. Remove chicken from yoghurt and brown lightly in the butter-onion mixture. Add yoghurt and tomatoes and continue cooking over a medium heat. Stir constantly until meat is brown and dry. Dissolve bouillon cube in 3 cups boiling water and pour over chicken. Let simmer gently on a low heat until chicken is tender, add more water if necessary. About 10 minutes before chicken is done, squeeze lime juice over it. Serve with side dish of chutney and pickles. Serves 6-8.

Overleaf: Kunan Yin, Goddess of Mercy, Hong Kong

Kokoda and Chicken in Pineapple

NASI GORENG

1 chicken
1 leek
1 parsley root
1 bay leaf
salt
3 cups long grain rice
2 cups oil
2 onions, sliced
4 cloves garlic
1 can crab meat
250g lobster tails
120g boiled ham, in strips
1 teaspoon caraway seeds,
    chopped
1 red pepper, in strips
1 knife-tip of mace
1 tablespoon peanut butter

Skin chicken and boil with leek strips, parsley root, bay leaf and salt. When chicken is done, pour off bouillon and retain it. Remove chicken meat from bones and cube. Wash rice repeatedly until water remains entirely clear, then boil it in chicken bouillon for about 20 minutes. When the grains have finished swelling, pour off cooking water. Heat oil in a saucepan and brown sliced onions and garlic in it. Add rice and simmer, stirring constantly, until it browns and all of the water has steamed away. Mix in crab meat, lobster tails, ham strips, caraway, pepper strips, mace, peanut butter, and last of all the pieces of chicken. Heat. Serve with shredded coconut and spicy sauces. Serves 4-6.

BARBECUE-STYLE ROAST DUCK

1.75kg roasting duck
1 clove garlic, crushed
1 teaspoon fresh ginger,
    finely grated
1 teaspoon hoi sin sauce
1 teaspoon sesame paste
1 teaspoon salt
1 tablespoon honey
1 tablespoon light soy sauce
½ teaspoon pepper

Wash duck inside and out, remove neck and giblets and reserve for making stock. Combine all other ingredients in a small saucepan and heat gently until honey melts and all ingredients are smoothly incorporated. Simmer for 2 minutes, adding a spoonful of water if it seems too thick, and use as marinade. Rub marinade all over duck, inside and out. Reserve remaining marinade to serve as a sauce. After 1 hour, place duck in oven bag or wrap in foil. (If using oven bag, follow manufacturer's instructions and do not fail to make 3 or 4 holes in top of bag near the tie.) Turn duck breast-downwards in roasting pan and cook in a moderate oven for 45 minutes. Turn duck breast-up and cook for a further 45 minutes to 1 hour. Remove from bag, carve duck and serve hot with reserved marinade. Serves 4.

CHINESE PARSLEY DUCK

2.5kg duckling
¼ cup soy sauce
1 teaspoon rice wine
1 cup peanut oil (for frying)
1 cup soy sauce
1 teaspoon anisette or kummel
60g bamboo shoots
6 water chestnuts, shredded
32g Chinese black mushrooms,
    shredded
30g mashed Chinese parsley
1 teaspoon light soy sauce
handful Chinese parsley

After thoroughly cleaning duck, rub the entire body for 5 minutes with ¼ cup soy sauce and rice wine. Crack backbone and fry duck in peanut oil until brown. Remove from oil and place in a deep pan with 1 cup of soy sauce, anisette, and enough water to cover. Allow to simmer until tender, turning occasionally. Remove and cool. Retain cooking water. If desired, extract the backbone. Place duck in bowl with 3 cups of sauce from deep pan and steam for 20 minutes. Shred vegetables and cook in a saucepan with juice from steaming. With a little water make a paste of the cornflour and add with light soy sauce to the vegetable sauce. Simmer for 2 minutes. Pour boiling sauce over duck and sprinkle with Chinese parsley. Serve with moi cheung (plum sauce). Serves 4-6.
Note: All dried vegetables must be cleaned and soaked until soft.

Aitutaki, Cook Islands

Previous page: Chicken in Crisp Noodle Basket and Cucumber Salad

WILD DUCK IN CASSEROLE

1 duck
1 clove garlic
butter
2 tablespoons brown sugar
3 rashers bacon
1 bay leaf
sprig of rosemary
½ green pepper, chopped
2 onions, chopped
3 tomatoes, sliced
3 tablespoons oil
½-1 cup red wine

Joint duck, rub with cut clove of garlic. Brown pieces in butter, remove to casserole dish and sprinkle with brown sugar. Add rest of the ingredients and cook in a moderate oven, 175°C, for 1 hour. Serves 4.

KIWI DUCK WITH SAVOURY RICE

1 duckling
115g butter
115g sugar
1¼ cups red wine
2 bay leaves
4 kiwifruit, sliced
1¼ cups demi-glace
150ml cream
2 oranges, segmented

For savoury rice:
1 small onion
1 cup rice
chicken stock

Prepare duckling by removing bones and cutting into bite-sized pieces. Heat pan and sauté duckling in butter until lightly brown. Add sugar, red wine, bay leaves, most of the kiwifruit and cook until tender. Remove duck from the juice, add demi-glace to pan and reduce until mixture thickens. Finish with cream. Arrange duckling on bed of rice in a serving dish. Place slices of kiwifruit on top and surround with oranges. Serves 2-4.

Savoury Rice:
White stock should always be 1¾ times the rice used. For the amount described in the recipe use ½ teaspoon salt, ¼ teaspoon pepper, 1 bay leaf. Finely chop the onion and fry in butter until transparent – do not brown. Add washed rice and stir for about 5 minutes over heat until the butter has coated each grain of rice. Add the boiling stock and place in 200°C oven for exactly 17 minutes, covered with a piece of buttered greaseproof paper and a lid.

DUCK WITH PINEAPPLE

3 pineapple rings
400g duck meat, boned and cubed
200ml sherry
120ml water
2 tablespoons soy sauce
1 teaspoon sugar
½ teaspoon monosodium
   glutamate
2 tablespoons pineapple syrup
1½ teaspoons cornflour
8 cherries

Divide each pineapple ring into 4 pieces. Cook duck in a saucepan with sherry and water for 20 minutes. Add the soy sauce, sugar, monosodium glutamate, pineapple syrup and cornflour mixed with a little water. Stir until boiling and boil for 5 minutes. Add pineapple and cherries and cook for about 1 minute. Remove to a heated dish and serve hot. Serves 4.

FRUIT-FILLED WILD DUCK

1-1.5kg wild duck
1 teaspoon salt
¼ teaspoon pepper
⅛ teaspoon ginger, grated
½ lemon
2 apples, quartered
1 orange, quartered
1 onion, quartered
2 slices bacon
1 cup orange juice

Singe and clean duck. Cut out oil sac at base of tail, cut off neck at body, leaving on the neck skin. Rinse and dry. Rub cavities of duck with a mixture of salt, pepper and ginger. Rub surface of duck with cut side of lemon. Fill cavities with apples, orange and onion. Close openings with skewers. Place duck breast-side up on a rack in roasting pan. Lay bacon over breast and pour over orange juice. Roast uncovered at 190°C for 1-1½ hours. Baste with pan gravy. Serves 2-4.

CASSEROLE OF PHEASANT

1 x 450g pheasant
4 leeks
2 onions, chopped
2 carrots, chopped
2-3 sausages
flour

Place prepared pheasant in baking dish and bake in the oven at 180°C for 30 minutes, basting frequently with fat. Remove and place bird in a casserole dish. Add juice from roasting dish and vegetables. Cover and bake at 160°C for 1 hour or until bird is cooked.
About 15 minutes before the end of cooking time add sausage balls made by skinning sausages, dividing each into half and rolling in flour. Serves 2.

PHEASANT NORMANDY

1 pheasant
90g butter
500g apples
150ml cream
salt and pepper

Prepare bird for roasting. Melt butter in pan, add pheasant and brown on all sides. Peel, core and slice apples thinly. Place half of the apples in a deep casserole dish, pour over a little of the melted butter and place pheasant on top. Surround with remaining apples. Pour rest of butter and the cream on top, season, and cover tightly. Cook in a slow oven, 175°C, for 1-1½ hours. Serves 2.

ROAST GOOSE WITH APPLE AND PRUNES

1 goose (about 4.5-5.5kg)
1 small onion, halved
salt and pepper
1kg apples, peeled and cored
250g prunes, soaked and pitted
juice of 1 lemon

For pan gravy:
1 teaspoon flour
6 teaspoons red wine

Wash cleaned goose thoroughly in hot water. Wipe with a clean cloth and rub goose inside and out with onion halves. Sprinkle with salt and pepper. Dice apples. The prunes should be soaked for several hours and pitted. Stuff goose with mixture of apples, prunes and lemon juice and sew or skewer the opening. Place goose in roasting pan, breast-up and roast in oven at 180°C allowing 40-50 minutes per kilogram. Baste every 15 minutes with pan drippings. After 1½ hours season again with salt and pepper. Continue roasting until golden brown.
Make up pan gravy by adding flour to the pan and stirring it into a thick gravy. Boil for a minute then add red wine and stir well. Remove bird and discard stuffing as the goose has by now absorbed the flavour of the fruit. Serve with the pan gravy. Serves 2.

MUTTONBIRD SUPREME

1 muttonbird
white sauce
2 tablespoons white wine

Place plucked and drawn muttonbird in pan, cover with water and bring to boil. Boil for a few minutes then drain and cover with new water. Repeat this procedure until bird is soft. Place under grill and cook until golden brown. Serve with a white sauce to which wine has been added. Serves 1.

ROAST TURKEY

4.5-7kg turkey, cleaned and drawn
salt
8-12 cups chestnut stuffing
10 strips bacon
2 cups vegetable stock or water

Rub entire surface and lightly sprinkle inner cavity of turkey with salt. Stuff turkey loosely, only partially filling cavity as stuffing will expand. If desired, skin around the breast may be lifted and also stuffed. By inserting a thin layer of stuffing under breast skin, the flavour is improved. Sew or skewer openings. Lay strips of bacon over the turkey, on the breast and legs especially since they brown readily. Or, instead of the bacon strips, arrange a double layer of cheesecloth saturated in melted fat over the bird, with the cloth hanging in the roasting pan. Truss bird by tying wings close to the body and putting the legs down and tying to tail-piece. This will keep the bird from drying out too quickly and make it easier to handle and turn. Place 2 cups of water or vegetable stock (prepared by cooking soup greens such as celery, parsley, etc) in a roasting pan and lay bird breast-down in pan. Set pan in oven preheated to 160°C. When half cooked, turn turkey over and complete roasting. Allow 30-50 minutes per kilogram of turkey, a longer time for old birds. Baste frequently with pan drippings, adding more hot water when necessary. A 7kg turkey serves 12-16; 4.5kg serves 8-10.

For chestnut stuffing:
1kg chestnuts
½ cup mushrooms, sliced
1 onion, sliced
250g butter
turkey liver and heart
1 dried bread roll
½ cup milk
3 eggs, separated
½ teaspoon nutmeg
½ cup sweetened cream
1 teaspoon salt
pepper

Boil chestnuts and remove skins. Sauté mushrooms and onion in part of the butter for about 5 minutes. Mince chestnuts. Chop liver and heart. Soak roll in milk and remove excess milk. Pass all ingredients through a sieve. Add egg yolks, remaining butter, nutmeg, cream, salt and pepper. Work with wooden spoon to a smooth paste. Finally, add the stiffly beaten egg whites. Mix and stuff turkey.

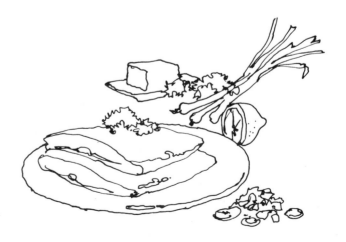

ROAST SWEET AND SOUR TURKEY

600g turkey meat
1 cup oil
2 tablespoons sugar
½ cup wine vinegar
1 knife-tip ground cloves
1 knife-tip ground cinnamon
1 knife-tip mustard powder
½ teaspoon garlic salt
1 onion, cubed
1 teaspoon salt
1 knife-tip ground white pepper
1 knife-tip cayenne pepper
2 tablespoons paprika
1 cup olive oil

It is best to use leg and breast meat for this dish. Fry turkey pieces in hot oil, turning down heat after 10 minutes and cooking meat for 20 minutes more. Remove bones by making small incisions in the meat. Bring sugar and vinegar to the boil with cloves, cinnamon, mustard, garlic salt, onion and salt. Blend in pepper, cayenne, paprika and oil. Simmer turkey in this creamy sauce for 15 minutes more and serve with potato crisps or garlic bread. Serves 4-6.

LAMB

LEG OF LAMB AOTEAROA

('Aotearoa', meaning The Land of the Long White Cloud, was the name the first Maori settlers gave to New Zealand.)

1 medium-sized leg of spring lamb
5 tablespoons honey
100ml white wine
oil
1 large onion, coarsely chopped
1 celery stick, sliced
1 large carrot, sliced
salt and pepper
300-400ml beef stock
pinch of mixed herbs

Remove shin from leg and trim off excess fat. Take honey and mix with white wine. With a syringe, inject wine and honey mix into the leg in several places. Rub a little oil onto leg and place in container, covering with onions, celery and carrots. Seal container and keep refrigerated for about 6-8 hours. Remove meat from vegetables, season and cook in moderate oven until half-done. Then add vegetables and finish cooking. Remove leg, keep warm. De-glace roasting residue with beef stock, bind lightly with beurre manié, bring to boil, strain and serve with meat. Serves 4-6.

STUFFED SADDLE OF LAMB

½ onion, chopped
3-4 mushrooms, chopped
butter
pinch of mixed herbs
150g minced lamb
3 bread rolls soaked in water and
    squeezed out
salt and pepper
1 egg
1 tablespoon parsley, chopped
1 saddle of lamb, boned
garlic oil

Sauté onion and mushrooms in butter. Add mixed herbs, minced lamb and squeezed bread rolls. Season to taste then add egg and parsley. Season saddle of lamb with a little garlic oil, salt and pepper. Fold stuffing into saddle, roll tightly and tie up with string. Make sure both ends are properly closed or stuffing will come out during roasting. Roast slowly, at 190°C-200°C, until well done. Serves 3.

STUFFED LOIN OF LAMB

1 shoulder or leg of lamb
salt and pepper
6 slices white bread (without crusts)
1 onion, chopped
2 teaspoons parsley, chopped
1 small bay leaf, chopped
¼ cup cream
thyme
3 slices cooked ham
1 egg
6 mushrooms, chopped

Bone lamb and season well. Soak bread in water or milk and press out well. Sauté onion and chopped bay leaf. Then mix in bread, parsley, cream, thyme, ham, egg and mushrooms to a fairly thick paste. Spread lamb with this filling, roll up neatly and tie with string. Cook in a moderate oven (180°C) for 1½-2 hours. Serves 4-6.
Note: A good sauce for this dish is a medium-thick mixture of tomato sauce with lager beer.

LEG OF LAMB À LA BONNE FEMME

leg of lamb, about 1kg
1 clove garlic
salt and pepper
100g butter
2 slices of bacon, chopped
12 small onions or shallots
1 large carrot sliced thinly into
    matchsticks
parsley ⎱ if using fresh spices
bay leaf ⎰ tie together,
thyme   otherwise tie in a
rosemary ⎰ small piece of cloth
¼l white wine
¼l stock
1 tablespoon tomato paste
a little flour or cornflour

Cut a few notches into leg of lamb and place a little pressed garlic in the notches. Season with salt and pepper. Melt most of the butter and, in a deep frying pan, simmer chopped bacon and onions for 10 minutes, then remove from pan. Increase heat and brown leg of lamb in pan. Reduce heat, add more butter, carrots, tied herbs and part of the white wine. Simmer for about 1 hour (if meat is too red for your taste, simmer longer). Gradually add more of the white wine and after 50 minutes the chopped bacon and onions.

Remove leg of lamb and keep warm. Add rest of the white wine, the stock and tomato paste. Simmer for 10 minutes and thicken with flour or cornflour. Serve with boiled potatoes, string beans, or buttered carrots and peas and a red wine. Serves 4.

ROAST LAMB ISLAND STYLE

2.5kg leg of mutton or lamb
salt and pepper
1-2 cloves garlic
2cm piece ginger
700ml soy sauce
700ml oil
1 cup pineapple, finely chopped
1 cup water or mild beef or
    chicken stock

Remove most of the surplus fat from the leg of mutton or lamb and score surface crosswise 5mm deep. Rub with salt and pepper and place in baking dish with lid. Crush garlic, ginger and mix with the soy sauce and oil. Beat or blend sauce until all ingredients are well combined. Pour over the leg. Spread pineapple over lamb, cover and place in an oven at 180°C. Cook for about 2½ hours, basting frequently. It may be necessary to add 1 cup water to the pan to retain moisture. Remove lid for the last 30 minutes of cooking. Serve with gravy from pan dripping. Serves 4.

LAMB RACK HAWKES BAY

3 racks of lamb, about 350g each
salt and pepper
juice of 3 oranges
3 tablespoons honey
3 tablespoons cointreau
350ml demi-glace
a few orange segments for garnish

Season lamb racks and cook in oven to medium rare, basting continuously with half the mixture of orange juice and honey. Remove meat and pour off excess fat. De-glace with rest of orange juice and honey mixture and cointreau. Add demi-glace, reduce, and pour over meat. Garnish with orange segments. Serves 6.

FRIED LAMB SWEETBREADS

3 or 4 lamb sweetbreads
salt-vinegar water
flour, seasoned with salt & pepper
2 eggs, beaten
2 cups hard bread roll-crumbs
85g butter or margarine
lemon quarters

Place sweetbreads in water and after soaking for 2 hours pull off outer membranes. Bring to boil in salt-vinegar water and simmer until done, about 10 minutes, then return to plenty of cold water. Drain cooled, firmed sweetbreads on kitchen cloths and press lightly, in the cloths, between two plates. Split in half lengthways and spread out. Dry all sides with flour, pour on beaten eggs and lightly roll in bread roll-crumbs, pressing these on to the surface well. Fry sweetbreads in a generous amount of butter until golden brown. Garnish with lemon quarters and serve some madeira or red wine sauce separately. Serves 4.

JAVANESE LAMB

1 teaspoon caraway seeds, minced
pinch of saffron filaments
1 red pepper grated
4 cloves garlic
1 teaspoon coriander grains,
    minced
salt
1 tablespoon oil
1 leg of lamb, boned & cut into large
    cubes
1 tablespoon wine vinegar
70g margarine
1 cup brandy
1 tablespoon curacao
1½ cups water
½ cup peas
½ cup green pepper

Prepare a spice mixture with the caraway, saffron, red pepper, garlic, coriander, salt and oil. Mix in an earthenware bowl. Rub pieces of lamb thoroughly with this mixture then soak meat in the vinegar for a few hours, preferably in a warm place. Drain meat and brown in a pan with hot margarine. Add brandy and curacao and reduce by half. Pour on water and simmer meat until done, along with the peas and green pepper. Serve this dish with fluffy rice, green beans and spinach as vegetables. Serves 6.

HOGGET ENGLISH STYLE WITH CAPER SAUCE

2-3kg hogget
4-6l water
2 onions
4 cloves garlic
800g carrots
1 bay leaf
1 bouquet garni
1kg french beans

For sauce:
½ onion, chopped
60g butter
80g flour
900ml clear veal stock or any
    meatstock
100ml cream
lemon juice
pinch of salt
¼-½ cup capers, chopped

Place hogget in salted water and cook for 2-3 hours depending on quality. Push garlic cloves into onions and boil with carrots, bay leaf and bouquet garni in the water.
To make sauce, sauté chopped onion in butter, add flour (do not brown mixture), then the boiling stock. Stir vigorously until sauce is smooth and simmer for 30 minutes (the longer it's cooked, the better it is). Strain sauce through fine sieve and add cream, salt, a little lemon juice and the chopped capers.
Slice cooked hogget, arrange slices on a platter, garnishing with beans, onions and carrots and pour sauce over. Serves 8-10.

SYDNEY SHISH KEBAB

1 tablespoon olive oil
½ teaspoon sugar
juice of 1 lemon
salt
freshly ground black pepper
500g lamb or mutton
12 pieces of green pepper
125g lean smoked bacon, sliced
8 slices of orange, peeled
2 onions, thickly sliced
oil for frying

Combine olive oil, sugar, lemon juice, salt and pepper in a bowl; beat thoroughly with rotary beater. Cut the meat in cubes, add to the bowl and marinate for several hours, turning meat frequently.
When ready to cook, insert meat on skewer, alternating with pieces of green pepper, bacon slices and thick slices of oranges and onions. Brush again with oil and cook on a grill over an open fire or under broiler heat. Serves 4.

Paella and Gazpacho

MARINATED MUTTON

1 leg of mutton with leg bones
   chopped off
1 large onion, halved
1 onion, sliced
1 bay leaf
1 cup milk
3 tablespoons flour
340g drained capers
a little lemon juice
salt and pepper

For marinade:
2 cups vinegar
water
4 cloves garlic, crushed
12 peppercorns, crushed
4 cloves
1 bunch cooking herbs
1 teaspoon salt

Remove all skin and fat from mutton and rub with the onion. Prepare enough marinade to completely cover meat and marinate for 24 hours, turning periodically. Remove, dry and boil in salted water with onion and bay leaf for 2 hours. The scum which forms must be skimmed frequently. Remove mutton as soon as it is cooked through. Boil down bouillon and beat it up with milk and flour. Season with capers, lemon juice, salt and pepper. Cut meat from bones and pour caper sauce over the thick slices. Serves 6-8.

SOUR LEG OF MUTTON

1 leg of mutton
200g bacon rashers
margarine
1 cup breadcrumbs (preferably
   white)
400ml sour cream
pepper
ground paprika
1 bunch parsley
1 bunch chives

For marinade:
450ml buttermilk
450ml vinegar
1 bay leaf
2 carrots, diced
2 onions, sliced
12 peppercorns, crushed
1 teaspoon salt
1 teaspoon sugar

Remove bones, fat and skin from leg of mutton. Then prepare marinade in a large earthenware pot. Cover leg in marinade and soak for several days. Remove and dry leg, then lard with strips of bacon and brown all over in the oven, basting with margarine. Pour on several spoons of marinade and place in oven heated to 200°C, reducing to 175°C after ½ hour. Cook for 1½ hours. Make a creamy gravy by adding breadcrumbs, sour cream and remaining ingredients to pan juices. Serve with potato salad. Serves 6-8.

Westland National Park, New Zealand

LAMB ITALIENNE

1kg lean lamb cut from leg
seasoned flour
2 tablespoons oil
1 clove garlic, crushed
2 onions, sliced
3 or 4 sticks celery, chopped
1 teaspoon salt
1 teaspoon sugar
1 cup beef or chicken stock
2 tablespoons tomato purée
½ cup white wine
¼ teaspoon rosemary
115g mushrooms, sliced
chopped parsley

Cut meat into pieces and coat with seasoned flour. Heat oil in saucepan, add meat, garlic, onions, chopped celery and salt and sauté until meat is well browned. Add sugar, boiling stock, tomato purée, wine and rosemary. Bring to boiling point, cover and simmer slowly for about 1¼ hours. Add mushrooms and cook a further 10 minutes. Serve hot sprinkled with parsley. Serves 5-6.

NEW ZEALAND LAMB SURPRISE

1 boned lamb loin and 1 fillet lamb
salt and pepper
340g can of apple juice
4 cooked lambs' tongues
8 apples, peeled
190g gruyère cheese, finely sliced
apple brandy
1 onion, chopped
1 green pepper, chopped
1 cup white wine
demi-glace
fresh cream
42g clarified butter
28g sugar

Season lamb with salt and pepper and pour over a little of the apple juice. Cut tongues into thin strips and mix with 3 of the apples and 60g of the cheese. Set loin in baking dish and make an incision down the meaty side of the loin to form a pocket. Place some of the cheese, apple and tongue mixture into pocket and along the loin. Place some more of the mixture in a pocket in the fillet and roll the fillet up inside the loin and tie. Season outsides. Brown loin and flame with apple brandy, place in oven for 25 minutes at 190°C.

Cut 4 apples into 1cm thick slices, cook in butter and sugar then place remaining cheese slices on and grill. Sauté chopped onion, 1 apple and green pepper and put aside.

Remove lamb. De-glace pan with white wine, apple juice and demi-glace and strain into apple, onion and green pepper mixture. Add cream to required sauce consistency. Adjust seasoning. Arrange apples and slices of lamb on a tray, sauce in a sauce-boat. Garnish and serve. Serves 4-6.

DURHAM LAMB CUTLETS

230g cold cooked lamb
1 small onion, chopped finely
15g butter
230g potato, mashed
1 tablespoon parsley, chopped
1 teaspoon tomato purée
salt and pepper
3-4 tablespoons flour
1 egg, beaten
5-6 tablespoons white breadcrumbs
fat for deep frying

Mince or chop lamb very fine. Cook onion in melted butter until golden brown. Add mashed potato and meat to onion, then chopped parsley and tomato purée. Season to taste. Cook altogether for a few seconds then turn mixture out onto a plate to cool. Divide into 8 equal-sized portions and shape into 'cutlets'. Roll each in flour then dip into beaten egg until coated all over. Roll in dried breadcrumbs.

Heat fat in a deep-fat frying pan. When fat is smoking slightly, place 3-4 cutlets into frying basket and lower into hot fat. Cook until cutlets are a rich brown. Drain on paper towel and keep warm while frying remaining cutlets. Arrange in an overlapping circle around a hot dish, and serve with vegetables and a brown or tomato sauce. Serves 4.

GRILLED ORIENTAL LAMB CHOPS

12 lamb steaks or round-bone lamb
  chops

For sauce:
2 onions, sliced
2 tablespoons coriander, ground or
  6 sprigs fresh coriander, plus
  1 tablespoon coriander, ground
2 cups yoghurt
2 teaspoons salt
2 teaspoons cumin, ground
1½ teaspoons black pepper
1½ teaspoons cloves, ground
1½ teaspoons cardamom, ground
1 teaspoon ginger
1 teaspoon cinnamon
1 teaspoon poppy seeds
2½ tablespoons melted butter
  (clarified if possible)
6 tablespoons lemon juice

Place onions, coriander, yoghurt, salt, cumin, pepper, cloves, cardamom, ginger, cinnamon, poppy seeds, melted butter and lemon juice in a blender and blend until smooth. Place chops in a shallow pan, spoon over half of the marinade and marinate, refrigerated, overnight. Then grill chops until cooked to your liking. Baste occasionally with the sauce. Heat leftover marinade and serve it as a sauce over the meat. Serves 12.

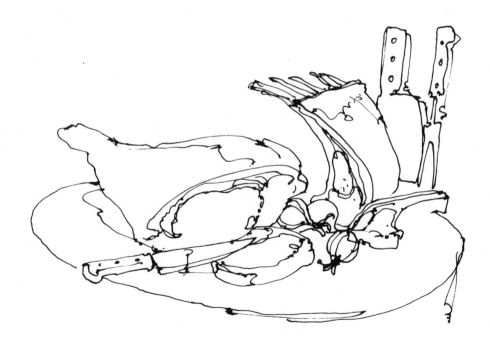

BEEF

SPANISH STEAKS

4-6 sirloin steaks, 2.5cm thick
8 tablespoons olive oil
4 tablespoons dry white wine
1 tablespoon lemon juice
2 tablespoons onion, coarsely
   chopped
2 cloves garlic, chopped
¼ level teaspoon oregano
¼ level teaspoon bay leaves,
   crumbled
1 tablespoon parsley, chopped
salt and freshly ground black pepper

Pierce steaks with thick barbecue skewer. Combine remaining ingredients and brush steaks with this mixture, forcing mixture well down into holes in meat. Allow meat to marinate for at least 2 hours in mixture before cooking. To grill, rub hot grid with a piece of suet, place steaks on grid and brush with marinade. Grill for 5 minutes on each side for a rare steak, a few minutes longer for medium-rare. Serves 4-6.

FILLET STEAK ALOHA

6 x 150g fillet steaks
6 pineapple slices

For marinade:
½ cup soy sauce
1 clove garlic
a 10mm piece of ginger
2 cups pineapple juice
⅓ cup oil

For sauce:
350ml demi-glace
1 cup red wine
salt and pepper

Marinate steaks in marinade for about 6 hours. Reserve marinade and cook meat to rare or medium-rare. Make up sauce from reduced marinade to which is added demi-glace, red wine and seasoning. Pour over meat and garnish with fine pineapple slices. Serves 6.

TERIYAKI STEAK

1 whole fillet of beef (about
   800-900g)
1 cup undiluted beef consomme
   (½ cup red or white wine with ½
   cup of water can be used instead)
⅓ cup soy sauce
1½ teaspoons seasoned salt
¼ cup onion, chopped
1 clove garlic
3 tablespoons lime juice
2 tablespoons sugar or honey

Slice meat into 1cm strips cutting across grain. Refrigerate in a marinade made by combining beef consomme, soy sauce, seasoned salt, onion, garlic, lime and sugar or honey. Drain meat and save marinade. Grill meat very quickly over a very hot grill, basting meat frequently with marinade. Serves 4-6.

CHINESE FILLET STEAK

500g beef
2 tablespoons white wine
4 tablespoons tomato sauce
1 tablespoon chilli sauce
1 teaspoon sugar
1 teaspoon sherry
¼ teaspoon salt
tomato, parsley and pineapple
    for garnish

For marinade:
½ teaspoon salt
1 teaspoon bicarbonate of soda
1 teaspoon cornflour
½ teaspoon dry sherry
⅓ cup water
¼ cup oil

Slice beef finely into 5 x 5cm strips. Mix up marinade and marinate beef in this for 24 hours. Remove and pan fry beef until medium rare. Mix wine, tomato sauce, chilli sauce, sugar, sherry and salt together in another pan and heat. Add beef and stir together. Remove from heat and serve hot with garnishing of tomato, parsley and pineapple. Serves 4.

JAPANESE-STYLE STEAK

1kg sirloin steaks
¾ cup olive oil or other salad oil
½ cup wine vinegar
1 large onion, sliced
3 tablespoons soy sauce
2 cloves
2 bay leaves
juice of ½ lemon
¼ teaspoon freshly ground black
    pepper
3 tablespoons brown sugar

Remove fat from steaks and cut into serving-sized pieces. Combine olive oil, wine vinegar, onion, soy sauce, cloves, bay leaves, lemon juice, pepper and 1 tablespoon brown sugar. Pour over steaks and marinate at room temperature for about 2 hours; turn steaks once. When you are ready to cook, remove steaks from marinade and rub with remaining 2 tablespoons brown sugar. Grill over hot grill to your liking. Serves 4-6.

MEXICAN STYLE FRIED MEAT

5 cloves garlic, sliced
3 onions, cubed
80g butter or margarine
450g minced meat (½ beef and ½
    pork)
4 tomatoes, peeled and chopped
50g almonds, chopped
12 pimento-stuffed olives, minced
2 bananas, sliced
2 apples, sliced
2 tablespoons sultanas, chopped
1 knife-tip each of ground cloves
    and cinnamon
¼ teaspoon cayenne pepper
salt
juice of ½ lemon

Toss garlic with onions in butter. Do not brown onions. Spoon in the meat, the tomatoes, almonds, olives, bananas, apples, sultanas, cloves, cinnamon, cayenne pepper and salt. Push contents of frying pan back and forth with wooden spoon. Finally, sprinkle on lemon juice. Serve with butter toast. Serves 4.

ROAST BEEF FRIED RICE

1 cup peas
2 eggs
3 tablespoons peanut oil
1 clove garlic, diced
1 small onion, diced
1 cup roast beef, diced
4 cups cold cooked rice
2 tablespoons light soy sauce
salt and pepper

Defrost peas if frozen. Beat eggs with a little of the oil and cook in a hot pan like a pancake, flipping eggs over. Cook for a few minutes, remove, leave to cool then cut into fine strips. Heat remaining oil and stir fry garlic and onion for about 1 minute. Add beef and stir fry for 1 minute also. Add peas, rice, soy sauce, salt and pepper to taste and stir fry for a few minutes more. Mix in the egg strips well and serve hot. Serves 4.
Note: This dish may be served with oyster sauce if desired.

FILLET OF BEEF WAIKATO

2-3 spring onions, finely chopped
butter
100g raw scallops, diced small
3 eggs, beaten
30ml cream
salt and pepper
800-900g prime beef fillet, trimmed
5-6 bacon rashers
100g fresh button mushrooms,
   sliced
50ml red wine
10-20ml madeira wine
500ml demi-glace
6 grilled tomato halves
1 tablespoon chopped parsley

Sauté spring onions and scallops until nearly cooked then add beaten eggs to which cream and seasoning have been added. Stir until eggs start to set (keep mixture on soft side, like scrambled eggs). Remove from pan and cool.
Take fillet and cut a pocket into its whole length, but not cutting ends of fillet right through. Pound fillet on inside of cut to increase space. Season and fill with egg mixture. Wrap with bacon rashers with cut side of fillet facing upwards. Secure overlapping bacon rashers with toothpicks on both sides of fillet. (Ensure toothpicks go through cut of fillet as well.) Roast in oven to medium rare, basting with cooking juices. Remove from pan and keep warm. Pour off excess fat from pan, add mushrooms and de-glace with red wine and madeira. Add demi-glace, bring to boil then beat some butter flakes into sauce. Line serving dish with a little sauce, cut fillet into required portions and arrange on sauce. Garnish with grilled tomato halves and sprinkle with parsley. Serve rest of sauce separately. Serves 4-6.

BEEF AND GREEN PEPPER

500g fillet steak
1 teaspoon lemon juice
1 tablespoon soy sauce
1 egg white
1 clove garlic
1cm piece of green ginger
1 small onion, finely sliced
oil for frying
1½ cups green pepper, sliced
2 tablespoons cornflour
1 cup water
1 large tomato, thinly sliced
2 teaspoons sherry
1 teaspoon oyster sauce (optional)
1 beef cube
salt and pepper

Cut steak into thin slices across grain. Marinate for 1 hour in lemon juice, soy sauce and egg white. Crush garlic and green ginger and with onion stir fry in hot oil for 5 minutes. Add green pepper and beef to pan and stir fry for a further 5 minutes. Mix cornflour in the water. Add to beef with tomato, then sherry, oyster sauce, beef cube and salt and pepper to taste. Stir fry for 2 minutes or until sauce is thick and glossy. Serve with Chinese egg noddles or rice. Serves 4-6.

BEEF SATAY

400-500g tenderloin steak
2½ tablespoons sugar
1 teaspoon salt
6 baby red onions or 200g common
   onion
4 or 5 cloves garlic
15g stem ginger
2 tablespoons caraway seeds
1 teaspoon turmeric
½ teaspoon lemon grass or
   lemon rind
¼ cup peanuts, skinned and ground

For sauce:
¾ cup peanuts, skinned and ground
2½ tablespoons sugar
1 tablespoon tamarind, grated (or
   sour plum or apricot)
½ medium red onion, chopped
1 small chilli pepper, seeded and
   finely chopped
1 teaspoon anchovy paste
1 teaspoon salt
1 medium red onion, shredded
   thinly
2½ tablespoons coconut oil
⅔ cup water

Cut steak into slices 6cm long x 2.5cm thick. Sprinkle sugar and salt over beef slices and rub in well. Skin red onion, garlic and ginger and grate together. Add spices and mix well. Hand mix beef in spice mixture, add peanuts and leave for 20-30 minutes. To make sauce: mix together the peanuts, sugar and tamarind after it has been dissolved in 2-3 tablespoons water. Mix chopped red onion with chilli pepper, anchovy paste and the salt. Sauté shredded onion in coconut oil over a medium heat until light brown. Add onion-pepper mixture and stir. Cook for about 20 minutes or until oil and other ingredients begin to separate, at which point add peanut and tamarind mixture and pour in ⅔ cup water. Taste, adding salt if necessary. Cook over a low heat to form a thick sauce.

Take 15cm skewers and thread on slices of beef up half their length. Broil on a charcoal grill until done. Ensure both sides are exposed to heat and brush beef with mixture of two parts coconut oil and one part water. Arrange skewers of hot broiled beef on platter around a cup of the sauce. Serves 4.

SEMARANG STYLE SLICED BEEF

500g lean steak
1 onion, roughly chopped
4 cloves garlic, crushed
1 teaspoon coarsely ground black
   pepper
3 tablespoons dark soy sauce
2 tablespoons palm sugar or
   substitute
2 tablespoons peanut oil
2 ripe tomatoes, chopped

Use Scotch fillet, topside, rump or round steak for this dish. Buy it in one piece so that you can cut it into thin round slices. Beat slices out thinly with meat mallet, taking care not to break through them. Blend onion, garlic, pepper, soy sauce and sugar until smooth and marinate meat in this mixture for 1 hour (longer if it's refrigerated). Heat oil in a wok or large frying pan, add meat slices drained of marinade and fry over high heat until brown on both sides. Add remaining marinade and tomatoes and cook on medium heat, stirring frequently until gravy is thick and smooth and the meat tender, about 12 minutes. Serves 4.

RAROTONGAN BEEF

900g tenderloin
250g onions, shredded
3 tablespoons coconut oil
4 cups coconut milk
salt

For spice mixture:
1½ teaspoons chilli powder
½ teaspoon cloves, powdered
½ teaspoon black pepper
1 teaspoon cardamom
1 teaspoon cinnamon

Cut meat into small slices about 1cm thick. Add warm water to spice mixture and blend until sticky. Sauté onions in coconut oil, add spices and meat and continue cooking. Pour in coconut milk and season with about 2 teaspoons salt. Lower heat and simmer until meat becomes quite tender and broth has been reduced by half. Serve in a ring of rice. Serves 4-6.

BARBECUED SPARERIBS

1.6kg spareribs

For marinade:
6 tablespoons soy sauce
4 tablespoons wine
6 tablespoons tomato sauce
5 tablespoons pineapple juice
1 tablespoon thyme leaves
4-5 sage leaves
1 cup salad oil
dash of black pepper

Blend all marinade ingredients well. Marinate spareribs overnight, drain and dry, then return to marinade for a few hours. Drain once more and barbecue over charcoal or roast in oven. Serves 4.

BEEFROLLS À L'ALLEMAGNE

1kg beef rump steak
salt and pepper
8 hard-boiled eggs
2 onions
250g ham, cubed
1 tablespoon chives, chopped
1 tablespoon chervil, chopped
1 tablespoon parsley, chopped
pinch of nutmeg
1 clove garlic, pressed
2 tablespoons flour
100g butter
½ tablespoon paprika
¾ cup red wine
500g fresh mushrooms, chopped
salt and pepper
chopped parsley

Trim fat from steaks, slice thinly (80-90g slices) and season with salt and pepper. Chop eggs and onions fine and mix with ham, chives, chervil, parsley, nutmeg and garlic. Divide mixture over beef slices. Roll beef into little rolls and tie with string. Flour beefrolls and brown in butter. When browned remove beefrolls, add rest of the flour and paprika and stir. Thin with red wine and a little water. Place beefrolls into mixture and simmer for 1 hour. Wash mushrooms and add to sauce in final 10-15 minutes of the cooking time. Season sauce with salt and pepper. Remove string from the rolls and serve in the sauce on a preheated oven dish with mashed potatoes (mashed with a little mustard). Garnish beefrolls with chopped parsley. Serve with watercress. Serves 4-6.

HAWAIIAN KEBABS

5cm piece fresh ginger, chopped
2 cloves garlic, chopped
2 small onions, chopped
1 cup soy sauce
4 tablespoons sugar
8 small chilli peppers, chopped
2 tablespoons red wine vinegar
4-5 teaspoons cornflour
½ cup water
1 kilo good quality sirloin cut into
　　bite-sized pieces

For shallot sauce: (for each skewer)
1½ teaspoons butter
2 tablespoons shallots, chopped
2 tablespoons dry red wine

In a small pan combine ginger, garlic, onions, soy sauce, sugar, chilli peppers and wine vinegar. Cook over medium heat until slightly thick (10-15 minutes). Blend cornflour and water and gradually stir into the sauce. Cook until clear and thick. Strain mixture and press out all juices. Discard pulp and let the sauce cool. Add beef pieces to sauce and marinate for 3-4 hours – keep pot covered. Thread 6-8 pieces of beef onto each skewer and grill on fairly high heat. Serve with shallot sauce. Sauté shallots until cooked but not browned. Add red wine and reduce until nearly all liquid is gone. Pour over skewers and serve immediately. Serves 4-6.

SPANISH MEATBALLS

1kg lean beef, minced
¼ onion, finely chopped
olive oil
4 tablespoons fresh breadcrumbs
2 level teaspoons salt
¼ level teaspoon thyme, rubbed
¼ level teaspoon cayenne pepper
1 bay leaf, crumbled
grated rind of ½ lemon
2 eggs, beaten
tomato or mushroom sauce

Place minced meat in a large mixing bowl. Sauté onion in olive oil until soft, add minced meat and mix well. Then add breadcrumbs, salt, thyme, cayenne, crumbled bay leaf and grated lemon rind. Mix well, adding eggs. Allow flavours to blend for 20 minutes then correct seasoning with additional salt, pepper, thyme or lemon rind (raw mixture should taste highly seasoned) and form into small balls the size of walnuts. Place meatballs in refrigerator to firm. When ready to serve sauté meatballs gently in olive oil until cooked through. Serve with a tomato or mushroom sauce. Serves 4-6.

VEAL WITH DILL SAUCE

1.4kg boned, rolled and tied
　　shoulder
4 white peppercorns
fresh dill
¾ tablespoon salt

For sauce:
28g butter
2 tablespoons flour
water or beefstock for slaking
a few drops beef extract
2 tablespoons dill leaves, chopped
1½ tablespoons wine vinegar
1½ tablespoons sugar
1 egg yolk, beaten
dill leaves for garnish

Place meat in boiling water and cook for 30 minutes, skimming off foam which forms. After 20 minutes cooking add whole peppercorns, dill twigs and salt. Prepare sauce: melt butter in a saucepan, stir in flour, then slake with enough water or beefstock to smooth sauce. Stir in a few drops of liquid beef extract, chopped dill leaves, wine vinegar, sugar and the beaten egg yolk. Quickly remove saucepan from heat to prevent egg from coagulating. Slice cooked meat. Pour this sauce over meat and decorate with dill leaves. Serves 4-6.

VEAL CREOLE

500g onions
olive oil
100g butter
1.3kg boned leg of veal
salt and pepper
½-1 cup white vinegar
1 cup cream

Slice onions finely and fry in oil and butter in a saucepan. Before onions change colour add veal, bound with twine to retain its shape. Brown veal with onions, turning it to brown evenly. Season with salt and pepper and pour in the vinegar. As soon as vinegar has evaporated, cover saucepan and lower the heat. Cook for 1½-2 hours. Check now and then on the thickness of the sauce. When onions are almost dissolved, remove from pan and sieve them. Place onion purée in a bowl with the cream and stir gently. Add mixture to the veal and cook quickly for 1 minute. Remove veal and cut into slices. Serve in a heated ovenproof dish and cover with the tasty sauce. Serves 4-6.

VEAL CUTLETS CORDON BLEU

4 thick veal cutlets
115g minced cooked ham
115g grated gruyere cheese
garlic salt
pepper
30g butter
30-45g flour
2-3 tablespoons oil
1 cup white wine
½ cup chicken stock
2 level tablespoons parsley and
    tarragon, both chopped

Cut a pocket in each cutlet from boneless side, being careful not to pierce the outer surface. Mix ham and cheese together, adding garlic salt and pepper. Melt half the butter and stir in. Stuff cutlets carefully, do not overfill. Seal openings with toothpicks, and roll cutlets in seasoned flour. Heat oil in pan, add remaining butter and when foaming fry cutlets – about 3 minutes to brown each side. Place in ovenproof dish. Add wine and stock to liquid in pan and bring to boil. Stir in chopped herbs. Pour sauce over cutlets and cook in oven preheated to 180°C until veal is tender, about 20-30 minutes. Serves 4.

PORK

CANADIAN CHRISTMAS PIE WITH PORK, VEAL AND CHICKEN

1kg chicken, par boiled, boned, and
   cut into pieces
salt and pepper
250g veal, ground
250g lean pork, ground
1½ teaspoons salt
¼ teaspoon pepper
2 cloves garlic, crushed
½ teaspoon allspice
½ cup water
1 cup onions, minced
1 tablespoon lard
1 egg yolk, beaten
1 teaspoon milk

For pastry dough:
2 cups flour
½ teaspoon salt
½ cup lard
⅓ cup butter
3 tablespoons iced water

Sprinkle pieces of chicken with salt and pepper. Season ground veal and pork with salt and pepper, garlic and allspice. Add water and mix well. Brown onions lightly in lard. Add ground meat and brown lightly for 5 minutes.

Line buttered baking dish with pastry dough made as follows: sift flour and salt, cut in lard and butter with two knives. Add water a few drops at a time. Continue cutting. Shape dough into a ball and chill for 1 hour. Roll out two thin crusts to line baking dish and top pie. Place pork and veal mixture at the bottom of pastry-lined dish and cover with a layer of chicken pieces. Cover with pastry dough. Cut slits into the upper crust to allow steam to escape and brush crust with mixture of the beaten egg yolk and milk. Bake in oven at about 190°C until crust is light brown. Reduce heat to 150°C and bake for 2 hours longer. The pie may be served either hot or cold. Serves 6-8.

ROAST PORK JAPANESE STYLE

2 tablespoons soy sauce
1 cup peeled and sliced shallots
1 teaspoon sugar
¼ teaspoon ground white pepper
1 tablespoon of juice or candied
   ginger
2 cloves garlic, grated
1 cup oil
700g cured pork scrags, cubed

Mix soy sauce with sliced shallots, sugar, pepper, ginger juice, garlic and oil, and marinate meat cubes in this mixture for 1 hour in a warm place, stirring frequently. Spread meat out on an oiled baking sheet and let roast in an oven at 250°C for about 45 minutes. Bring marinade to a boil in a saucepan and season to taste. Serve meat cubes separately and dip them in hot sauce as they are eaten. Serve with rice. Serves 4.

ITALIAN ROAST PORK

1 piece loin of pork (1.5-2kg)
3 fat cloves garlic
½ Spanish onion, finely chopped
   and mixed with 2 tablespoons
   olive oil
rosemary leaves
salt and freshly ground black pepper
2 bay leaves, crumbled
water

Remove rind and about half the fat from loin of pork. Cut each garlic clove into 4 slivers. Pierce pork loin in 12 places with a thick skewer and insert a garlic sliver, a little of the onion mixture and 3 to 4 leaves of rosemary in each hole. Rub meat with salt and pepper and crumbled bay leaves. Place in a roasting pan with about 3cm water. Roast meat in a preheated moderate oven, (190°C), for about 60 minutes per kilogram, or until the meat is tender and moist. Skim fat from pan juices and serve with pork roast. Serves 4-6.

ROAST PORK RIB

3 carrots
1.25kg pork fillet (with ribs)
salt
1 clove garlic
½ cup olive oil
85g butter
freshly ground pepper
½ cup white wine
½ cup chicory
milk

Cut carrots into thin strips. Pierce meat in several places with a sharp knife and insert strips of carrot and a little salt. Rub pork with clove of garlic, then tie it in several places to help it keep its shape. Cook pork in a saucepan with the oil and butter. Brown evenly over a high heat, season with salt and freshly ground pepper and pour in wine. When wine has evaporated, pour milk over roast and put it into a hot oven. Watch carefully during cooking, turning meat regularly and basting it with tablespoons of its own gravy. When cooked, cut pork neatly into slices, each slice with a rib-bone attached. Arrange slices of pork on a heatproof dish and pour the sauce over. Garnish with curls of chicory. Serves 4-6.

RED ROAST PORK

500g pork fillet
1 teaspoon five-spice powder
½ tablespoon soft brown sugar
1 teaspoon fresh ginger, very finely chopped
1 tablespoon hoi sin sauce
1 tablespoon soy sauce
1 clove garlic, crushed
peanut oil

Trim pork but leave it in one piece. Mix together remaining ingredients except the oil and combine them thoroughly. Place meat in a baking dish, brush with the oil and then coat in sauce mixture. Marinate pork for 1-2 hours, occasionally spooning more oil over the pork. Place on a rack in a roasting pan and roast in hot oven for 10 minutes. Reduce oven temperature to 190-200°C for further 35 minutes. Cut fillet into slices diagonally and serve on a plate of rice. Serves 4.

CRISP ROAST PORK

leg of pork, about 4-5kg
salt

Score the skin of the leg of pork with the point of a sharp knife at 5mm intervals. Pour boiling water over the leg. When dry, rub with salt. Put the pork in the oven at 240°C and cook for 2-2½ hours, or until done. Serves 15-20.

PORK CUTLET CALIFORNIAN

8 x 125g pork cutlets
55-75g flour
salt and pepper to taste
170g clarified butter
8 peach halves
170ml apricot brandy
8 slices white bread, toasted
8 slices smoked cheese
rice pilaf

Flatten each cutlet and dredge in flour seasoned with salt and pepper. In frying pan, sauté cutlets in butter, 3-4 minutes each side. Keep warm. Drain peach halves and sauté in same frying pan as cutlets for 3-4 minutes each side. Add apricot brandy and remove from heat. Arrange toast in a single layer in baking pan. Top each toast slice with a cutlet and peach half. Pour over remaining juices from frying pan then top each peach half with a slice of cheese. Bake in preheated 200°C oven for 10-15 minutes. Serve with rice pilaf. Serves 4.

SUCKLING PIG IN HORSERADISH SAUCE

2 carrots, chopped
1 parsley root, chopped
1 suckling pig
2 peppercorns
2 sprigs parsley
salt and pepper
4 tablespoons horseradish, grated
½ cup sour cream
pinch of sugar

Cover carrots and parsley root with water and cook for 1 hour. Strain and save liquid. Clean suckling pig and place whole in a large pan. Add strained broth of vegetables, peppercorns, parsley and enough water to cover pig. Bring to the boil and simmer for 2 hours or until meat is tender. Add salt and cook pig in the salted water. Drain and cut into serving portions. Mix horseradish with sour cream and add pinch of sugar, ½ teaspoon salt and pepper. Pour over meat. Serve cold. Serves 8-10.

FILLET OF PORK IN BEER SAUCE

2 cloves garlic
2 onions, cubed
2 pork loins, sliced
1 teaspoon ground paprika
100g butter
½ cup light beer
1 cup bouillon
1 cup each of shredded white
    cabbage, chopped carrots, and
    sliced green beans
½ cup sour cream
salt and pepper
cayenne pepper

Crush garlic to paste on chopping board and fry with onions, meat slices and ground paprika in butter. Turn often to brown all sides. Cook very quickly as the onion and garlic will burn easily: turn heat up high very briefly then turn down again. After 3-4 minutes slake contents of pan with beer. Add bouillon and vegetables then turn out into a baking dish. Cover and simmer in a hot oven for 30 minutes. Flavour pan juice with sour cream and season with salt, pepper and a dash of cayenne. Serves 4.

KONIGSBERG MEATBALLS

240g pork
240g bacon
2 tablespoons coarse sausage filling
2 onions
2 slices white bread
1 tablespoon capers
½ tablespoon anchovy paste
4 eggs
salt and pepper
pinch of paprika
1 teaspoon marjoram, ground
50g butter
2 teaspoons flour
½ cup cream
2 egg yolks
juice of ½ lemon
1 teaspoon sugar

Run meats through fine setting of grinder along with onions and softened slices of bread. Stir in capers, anchovy paste, eggs, salt, pepper, paprika and marjoram. Mix well. Using dampened hands, fashion meatballs. Place in boiling salted water and cook until done. Prepare a light roux sauce with the butter, flour and cooking liquid. Finish sauce with cream and egg yolks. Add lemon juice and sugar. Serve meatballs in a bowl with sauce. Serves 4-6.

CEVAPCICI

500g ground lean beef
500g ground lean pork
1 teaspoon salt
¼ teaspoon pepper
1 teaspoon paprika
1 egg, slightly beaten
1 large garlic clove, crushed
5 or 6 drops Tabasco sauce
1 teaspoon marjoram
3 to 4 tablespoons beef broth or
   bouillon

Combine all ingredients in a mixing bowl and lightly knead mixture to blend thoroughly. Form into finger-shaped sausages about 2cm thick and 10cm long. Cook slowly on a charcoal grill or under a grill until well browned. Turn sausages often as they cook. They are done when brown on outside and slightly pink inside. Serves 6.

CÔTE DE PORC BOLOGNA

2 x 150g pork chops
2 slices lean bacon
2 slices mild cheese
salt and pepper
flour
2 eggs, beaten
sauce milanaise
20g lean bacon, diced and fried in
   butter

Trim fat from chops and cut in half in such a way that the bone still keeps both sides together. Place bacon and cheese slices between the two sides and seal carefully. Season, dip in flour then in egg and fry slowly in butter until golden. Cover bottom of casserole dish with sauce milanaise, sprinkle diced bacon on top of sauce, place chops on top of this. Serve with noodles or rice. Serves 2.

LOIN FILLETS OF PORK WITH PRUNES AND CREAM SAUCE

24 dried prunes
500ml dry white and red wine
   (mixed)
750g pork (fully trimmed and boned
   rib end of loin, tied and sliced
   into 12 x 25mm thick noisettes)
salt and freshly ground back pepper
flour
75g butter
6 tablespoons vegetable stock
6 tablespoons cream
2 tablespoons redcurrant jelly
few drops lemon juice

Soak prunes in mixed wine at room temperature for 5 hours, turning occasionally. Cook over moderate heat for 10 minutes until tender. Drain. Reserve wine. Season pork noisettes with salt and pepper and coat finely with flour. Melt butter over moderate heat in large frying pan. When foam subsides, brown noisettes for about 5 minutes on each side until rich golden brown. Remove. Pour off most of the fat from the pan, leaving barely enough to cover the bottom. Add wine which the prunes were soaked in and boil quickly, uncovered, until almost evaporated. Pour in stock and bring to the boil again. Return noisettes to the pan, cover and simmer gently over moderate heat 35-45 minutes, until tender. Transfer noisettes to a deep, heated dish. Remove strings and place in oven to keep warm, (130°C).
Remove all fat from stock, pour in cream and bring to the boil. Boil sauce rapidly, stirring constantly, until moderately thick. Stir in prunes, jelly and lemon juice. Cook until jelly is dissolved and prunes heated through. Stir constantly. Season to taste. Lift out prunes and arrange them around noisettes. Spoon sauce over prunes and noisettes and serve at once. Serves 4-6.

WUN TON

For 'skins':
1 cup flour
½ teaspoon salt
1 egg
½ cup water

Sieve flour and salt together. Make a well in the centre, add egg and mix into flour. Gradually add in water a little at a time and mix into a dough. Roll dough out as thin as paper on a benchtop well dusted with flour. Cut pastry into 7.5 x 7.5cm squares. Dust squares with flour so that they won't stick together. Note: 'Skins' can be wrapped in foil and kept in the refrigerator for a week.

For stuffing:

6 Chinese mushrooms
230g pork meat, chopped
1 tablespoon chopped scallion or
    spring onion
1 teaspoon soy sauce
1 egg, beaten
12 wun ton 'skins'
salt and pepper
1 egg white

Wash and soak mushrooms until soft, then drain and chop. Mix pork, mushroom, scallion, soy sauce and egg together and place mixture in the centre of each of the wun ton 'skins'. Bring the four corners together and press together, sealing joint with egg white. Place wun ton in 10 cups water and bring to boil. Cook wun ton for about 5 minutes then remove, drain and run under cold water. Serves 4-6.
Note: Wun ton can be kept for a few days in the refrigerator.

LEG OF PORK WITH CASHEW NUTS

30g broccoli
120g cashew nuts, roasted
5 teaspoons sherry
¼ teaspoon salt
¼ teaspoon pepper
½ teaspoon monosodium glutamate
1 teaspoon cornflour
200g leg pork, diced
4 tablespoons peanut oil
1 carrot, boiled and diced
30g bamboo shoots, diced
2-3 chestnuts, diced
¼ onion, diced
2 tablespoons soy sauce
½ teaspoon sugar

Cut broccoli into suitable pieces. If cashew nuts are not roasted, fry first in oil until brown, then drain and keep crisp. Add 1 teaspoon sherry, salt, pepper, ¼ teaspoon monosodium glutamate and cornflour to the meat and mix well. Heat 2 tablespoons oil in a pan and fry meat until it's cooked and looks white in colour. Remove from pan. Add another 2 tablespoons oil to the pan, then carrot, bamboo shoots, chestnuts, broccoli and onion and cook for 2 minutes. Add pork, soy sauce, sugar and ¼ teaspoon monosodium glutamate. Stir well together for 1 minute, remove to a heated dish, sprinkle with cashew nuts and serve hot. Serves 4.

PORK AND BAMBOO SHOOTS

1kg lean pork, cubed
3 tablespoons soy sauce
1 tablespoon sherry
1 teaspoon ground ginger
1 teaspoon brown sugar
2½ cups water
115g bamboo shoots

Marinate pork in soy sauce, sherry, ginger and sugar for 20 minutes. Place pork and marinade in a large pan, add the water and bring to the boil. Cover and simmer for 1 hour, skim from time to time if necessary. Drain and finely shred bamboo shoots, add to the pan and simmer for 10 minutes. Thicken the mixture with cornflour diluted in cold water if desired. Season to taste and serve. Serves 6.

SWEET AND SOUR PORK

500g pork loin, diced
6 tablespoons cornflour
oil for deep frying
½ teaspoon garlic, chopped
1 small green pepper
1 cup pickled vegetable salad

For batter mixture:
1 egg yolk
1 tablespoon cornflour
1 tablespoon soy sauce

For sauce:
3 tablespoons vinegar
3 tablespoons sugar
3 tablespoons water
3 tablespoons tomato sauce
½ teaspoon salt

For thickening agent:
1½ teaspoons cornflour
1½ teaspoons water

Marinate pork in marinade of batter mixture for 20 minutes. Mix 6 tablespoons cornflour into marinade and coat pork before deep frying. Deep fry for 3 minutes, remove from fat, reheat fat to medium heat and re-cook pork for a further 3-4 minutes. Remove pork and drain.
Reheat pan and fry garlic, bite-sized pieces of green pepper and pickled salad for a few minutes. Add mixture of sauce recipe and bring to the boil. Make up thickening agent and add to pan. Mix in the pork, season and serve. Serves 4-6.

PORK AND MUSHROOM

500g lean pork
1 tablespoon soy sauce
1 tablespoon sherry
2 tablespoons oil
115g fresh mushrooms, sliced
1 teaspoon cornflour
3 tablespoons stock or water

Cut pork into thin slices and marinate in soy sauce and sherry for about 15 minutes. Remove and fry the meat in the oil over a fierce heat for a few minutes, stirring all the time. Remove pork slices from pan and keep hot. Quickly fry mushrooms in fat, add meat and mix together. Make up a thickening mixture with cornflour and stock and add to the pan. Stir and simmer a few moments then season and serve. Serves 4-6.

FRIED MEAT DUMPLINGS

4 cups flour
salt
½ cup cold water
1 cup boiling water
230g pork, minced
115g pork fat, minced
pinch of pepper
1 tablespoon spring onion, chopped
1 tablespoon sherry
1 teaspoon salt
1 teaspoon sugar
1 teaspoon soy sauce
1 cup green beans, finely diced
1 cup celery, finely diced
sesame oil
1 teaspoon cornflour

Sieve flour and a pinch of salt together. Divide flour in half and knead one half with cold water into a dough, the other with boiling water into a dough. Combine and cover with a wet towel. Mix together pork, pork fat and all other ingredients. Shape dough into a cylinder, cut into small pieces and roll out each piece into a small flat circle about 8cm in diameter. In the middle of each circle place a portion of the pork mixture. Fold the dough circle in half to form a half-moon shape and press the two ends together to seal in the pork. Arrange dumplings in a pan with a little oil and sauté, then add a little water, cover, and steam for a few minutes. Remove lid and add a little bit more oil and cook for a moment more. Remove onto grease-proof paper to drain. Serve with chilli sauce if desired. Serves 4-6.

Roast Pork Japanese Style and Cucumber Salad with Crab

SPRING ROLLS

230g minced pork
115g shrimps, peeled
1 tablespoon oil
2 scallions or spring onions
230g bean sprouts
oil for deep frying
1 tablespoon soy sauce
1 teaspoon salt
pinch of brown sugar
2 cups flour
2½ cups water
1 egg

Mix pork and shrimps together and fry in oil for 2 minutes. Wash and finely chop spring onions, drain bean sprouts and add both to the pork. Mix well and stir fry for 2 minutes. Stir in soy sauce, salt and sugar. Remove from heat. Mix flour, water and egg to a smooth batter. Using a heavy-based frying pan, lightly greased, make 16 very thin pancakes with the batter cooked on one side only. Place some of the mixture in the centre of each and fold over to form a half-moon shape. Seal edges with water and deep fry for 15 minutes. Serves 4-6.

BOILED PASTRY BALLS

230g lean pork
2 tablespoons soy sauce
1 teaspoon sherry
1 scallion or spring onion
few drops sesame oil
1 tablespoon cornflour
pinch of salt
2 cups rice flour
¾ cup hot water

Grind pork and mix in soy sauce and sherry. Chop scallion finely and add to pork with sesame oil, cornflour and salt. Mix well until blended. Combine flour and hot water together to make a soft dough, adding more water if necessary. Divide dough into 24 pieces and shape each into a ball. Make a hole in centre of each ball and press in a little of the pork filling. Shape dough around filling and pinch edges together. Drop balls into a large pan of salted boiling water and bring back to the boil for 5 minutes. Add 1¼ cups cold water to pan and bring back to the boil for another 3 minutes. Drain balls and serve. Serves 4-6.

FRIED NOODLES

500g noodles
30g dried mushrooms
85g shredded roast pork
85g shrimps
500g bean sprouts
85g scallion or leek, finely sliced
60g carrots, shredded
2 green and red sweet peppers,
    shredded
60g finely chopped shallots

Marinade
1½ teaspoons salt
2 teaspoons sugar
1 teaspoon black soy sauce
pinch of pepper
dash of sesame oil
dash of chilli oil
½ cup stock

Rinse and cook noodles in water and drain. Soak and shred mushrooms and cook. Marinate shredded pork in marinade mixture for 2-3 hours and stir fry in a little oil. Add shrimps, stir fry a few minutes more and remove. Sauté sprouts in hot oil, add scallion and mix together. Remove from pan. Sauté carrot strips and shredded peppers and remove. Sauté shallots in hot oil, add noodles and stir fry. Stir in all other ingredients and mix well. Season and pour in stock. Simmer for a moment, then serve. Serves 4-6.
Note: Sesame oil may be replaced with oyster sauce.

Muri Lagoon, Rarotonga

CRISPY PORK

500g lean pork
1¾ cups water
2 tablespoons soy sauce
1 tablespoon sugar
1 clove star anise
1 tablespoon sherry
pinch of monosodium glutamate
1 cup self raising flour
pinch of salt
1 egg
⅔ cup water
oil for frying

Cut pork into 2.5cm cubes and place in a saucepan with water, soy sauce, sugar, star anise, sherry and monosodium glutamate. Simmer until tender, about 45 minutes. Drain well. Sift flour and salt into a bowl, make a well in the centre, drop in the egg and mix with a wooden spoon, gradually bringing in the flour from around the edge. Add ⅔ cup water or more, gradually beating. Coat pork in batter and fry until golden. Drain well and serve. Serves 4.

CRISP FRIED PORK WITH SWEET SOUR SAUCE

500g pork fillets or pork chops
1 tablespoon light soy sauce
1 tablespoon Chinese wine or dry
  sherry
½ teaspoon salt
¼ teaspoon pepper
¼ teaspoon five-spice powder
1 cup flour
¾ cup warm water
1 tablespoon peanut oil
1 egg white
extra peanut oil for deep frying

For sweet sour sauce:
1 tablespoon light soy sauce
1 tablespoon Chinese wine or dry
  sherry (optional)
3 tablespoons tomato sauce
3 tablespoons vinegar
2 tablespoons sugar
¾ cup water
1 tablespoon cornflour
1 tablespoon water
1 small onion
2 tablespoons peanut oil
1 clove garlic, crushed
¼ teaspoon fresh ginger, finely
  grated
½ cup water chestnuts, sliced
1 red sweet pepper, diced
3 tablespoons peas
2 tablespoons preserved melon
  shreds, (optional)

If using pork chops, remove rind first then cut pork into 1cm wide slices, then into 2.5cm squares. Mix with soy sauce, wine, salt, pepper and five-spice powder. Refrigerate while preparing batter. Mix flour and warm water to a smooth batter with a wooden spoon, stir in oil and stand for 30 minutes. Beat egg white until stiff and fold in. Heat oil. Dip pieces of pork in batter and deep fry a few at a time over medium heat until pork is cooked and batter golden. Drain on absorbent paper and set aside. Make sauce.

Combine soy sauce, wine, tomato sauce, vinegar, sugar and water in a bowl and stir until sugar dissolves. Mix cornflour with about 1 tablespoon cold water to a smooth mixture. Peel onion, cut into four lengthways, then cut each quarter across into two. Separate layers of onion. Heat oil, add onion, garlic, ginger, water chestnuts, pepper and peas and fry for 2 minutes. Add combined sauce mixture, bring to a boil then stir in cornflour and cook, stirring constantly, until thickened. Remove from heat and stir in melon shreds.

Shortly before serving, reheat oil and once more fry pork, a few pieces at a time, on a high heat for just a few seconds. This second frying makes the batter very crisp. Drain on absorbent paper. When all the pork is fried arrange on a plate, pour hot sauce over and serve immediately. Serves 4-6.

CHILLI CHOP

85g shredded chicken
soy sauce
230g bean sprouts
oil for frying
1 dried mushroom
1 clove garlic, sliced
2 teaspoons butter
fresh chilli pepper, finely sliced
1 teaspoon Chinese white wine
115g shredded roast pork
115g shredded abalone
½ teaspoon salt
½ teaspoon sugar
dash of pepper
dash of sesame oil

Season chicken with a little soy sauce and allow to stand for about 15 minutes. Wash and drain bean sprouts, sauté in hot oil with salt and set aside. Soak and wash dried mushroom (don't soak too long or it will lose its flavour). Shred and steam or cook until soft. Sauté garlic in butter and remove. Add chilli to pan and sauté. Mix in chicken with a little wine and cook for a few minutes more. Add shredded roast pork, shredded abalone, bean sprouts and mushroom and fry thoroughly. Season with salt, sugar, pepper and sesame oil and serve hot. Serves 4-6.

CHINESE DRIED OYSTERS WITH PORK AND SEAWEED

250g dried oysters
250g pork tenderloin
½ cup soy sauce
1 teaspoon salt
1 clove garlic, crushed
¼ cup rice wine
1 cup peanut oil
15g fat choy (dried seaweed)
2 cups chicken broth
1 small piece chicken fat
2 tablespoons water
½ tablespoon cornflour

Soak oysters in cold water for 2 hours until soft. Bring oysters and water to the boil, strain and carefully clean all sand from oysters. Again bring oysters to the boil in a saucepan of water. Simmer for 10 minutes. Strain and save juice. Wash pork tenderloin and wipe dry. Soak the whole piece in soy sauce with salt, crushed garlic and wine for 5-10 minutes. Deep fry in hot oil until brown. Remove and run under cold water for 10-20 minutes. Slice into 5mm thick slices, about the size of oysters, and place alternate layers of pork slices and oysters into a bowl. Wash seaweed, cover with chicken broth and boil for 4 minutes with a piece of chicken fat. Strain and place on top of pork and oysters. With 2 tablespoons of water make a paste of cornflour. Add it to juice saved from oysters and bring to the boil. Pour boiling sauce on top of seaweed, pork and oysters and serve. Serves 4.

CANADIAN STYLE PIG'S FEET

6 small pig's feet, cut into pieces
2 cloves garlic, crushed
1 tablespoon salt
½ teaspoon pepper
¼ teaspoon nutmeg
¼ teaspoon cinnamon
¼ teaspoon ground cloves
4 tablespoons fat
2 onions, diced
1 carrot, quartered
1 bay leaf, crushed
boiling water
¾ cup browned flour

Rub each piece of meat with crushed garlic. Roll meat in salt, pepper and spices until each piece is well coated. Fry until quite brown in 4 tablespoons fat. Add onions, carrot, bay leaf and enough boiling water to cover meat. Simmer covered for 3½-4 hours until meat is almost falling off the bones. Thicken with browned flour by sifting it over meat. Boil for about 20 minutes longer. Serves 4.

BAKED PICKLED PORK

600-700g boiled pickled pork
cloves
8 slices pineapple
8 maraschino cherries
100ml lemon juice
100g sugar

Remove the rind and some fat from the boiled pickled pork. Score and decorate with cloves, pineapple and maraschino cherries. Brush with a mixture of lemon juice and sugar. Bake at 180°C until browned (not more than an hour). Serves 4.

PICKLED PORK

2.25*l* water
600ml beer
½ cup sugar
440g salt
2 bay leaves
6 peppercorns
2 teaspoons saltpetre (sodium
    nitrate)
3-5kg piece of pork

Bring water to the boil with the beer, sugar, salt, bay leaves, peppercorns and saltpetre. Simmer for 5 minutes. Allow to cool completely then pour brine over pork placed in a plastic or earthenware container. Weight the pork down so it is completely submerged in brine. Store in refrigerator. Pickle for 2½ days per 500g of pork. Turn every second day, making sure to stir up the brine as you do so. Remove and rinse. Cook by method given below. Serves 10-15.

Note: If there is not sufficient brine, add 90g of salt for every additional 500ml of water.

BOILED PICKLED PORK

pickled pork
2 teaspoons cloves
2 teaspoons black peppercorns
½ cup sugar

Tie piece of pickled pork in a cloth and place in a large pot with plenty of water. Add the cloves, peppercorns and sugar. Bring to boil then simmer 20 minutes per 500g of pork.

GAME

GRILLED WILD BOAR STEAK

6 x 200g boar steaks
salt and pepper

For sauce:
1 large red onion
250g large mushrooms
1 large sweet red pepper
50g fat
1 cup claret
bay leaf
sprig parsley
a few celery tops tied in a cotton bag
2 cloves garlic, crushed
½ cup clear stock
salt
cayenne pepper
½ cup redcurrant jelly
shot of brandy

First prepare the sauce, and keep it hot. Slice onion, mushrooms, and red pepper thinly, discarding seeds and core of pepper. Heat fat, add sliced vegetables and cook until soft but not browned, stirring constantly. Add claret, bay leaf, parsley and celery tops then the garlic and stock. Mix carefully and cook gently for 20 minutes. Add salt and cayenne pepper to taste, stir in the redcurrant jelly and finally the brandy. Discard the herbs and keep the sauce hot while the steaks are cooking. Sear steaks on both sides over or under a high-heat flame, then reduce the heat and grill to the required degree. Sprinkle each steak lightly with salt and pepper. Pour sauce over the steaks and serve with grilled tomatoes and pickled gherkins. Serves 6.

WILD RABBIT STEWED WITH PRUNES

1 wild rabbit
100ml vinegar
250ml red wine
1 bay leaf
a few juniper berries
2-3 cloves garlic, minced
3 cloves, crushed
butter for frying
2 tablespoons flour
200ml stock
450g prunes, soaked and pitted
salt and pepper
1 tablespoon redcurrant jelly

Clean rabbit and cut into neat pieces. Place vinegar, wine, bay leaf, juniper berries, garlic and cloves in bowl and add pieces of rabbit. Marinate for 24 hours. Remove rabbit pieces, drain and wipe dry. Strain marinade and keep. Heat butter and fry pieces of rabbit until golden brown. Stir flour into butter well and then gradually add the stock and 200ml marinade. Add prunes, salt and pepper and cook gently until rabbit is tender. Remove rabbit and prunes from pan and place onto hot serving dish. Strain sauce, return to pan and add redcurrant jelly. Bring quickly to boil and pour over rabbit and prunes. Serves 3.

CREAMED RABBIT

1 rabbit
2½ cups water
vinegar
120g bacon
1 onion, chopped
salt and pepper
30g flour
⅔ cup milk
1 cup mushrooms, chopped
parsley, chopped

Soak rabbit for several hours or overnight in water to which a little vinegar has been added to whiten the flesh. Remove and cut into neat pieces. Save marinade. Dice bacon, put into a pan with chopped onion, rabbit, seasoning and water. Cover and simmer gently for 1½ hours until tender. Blend flour and milk, stir mixture. Add chopped mushrooms and return to oven until gravy has thickened and mushrooms are cooked. Re-season as necessary and garnish with parsley. Serves 2-4.

RABBIT AND PRUNE CASSEROLE

1 rabbit
1¾ cups red wine
2 tablespoons vinegar
2 bay leaves
6 peppercorns
60g butter
120g prunes, pitted
45g flour
1 tablespoon redcurrant jelly
salt and pepper

Joint rabbit, place into a bowl with wine, vinegar, bay leaves and peppercorns. Leave overnight. Remove from marinade and wipe dry. Retain wine. Heat butter in a pan, add rabbit and cook for a few minutes, then remove to a casserole dish and add prunes. Stir in flour, cook for a few minutes, remove from heat and gradually add strained wine. Return to heat and simmer until thickened. Pour over rabbit. Cover casserole and cook at 175°C for about 2 hours. Just before serving stir in jelly and correct seasoning. Serves 2-4.

VENISON CASSEROLE

1kg venison
2 small onions, chopped
2 tablespoons butter
1 large can mushroom soup
2 tablespoons flour
½ teaspoon paprika
1 teaspoon salt
black pepper

Cut venison into pieces, roll in seasoned flour. Brown chopped onions in butter until golden, add venison and brown a few minutes more. Remove to a casserole. Pour soup over, cover and bake in a moderately slow oven, about 160° C, for 2 hours. Add a little water or stock if necessary. Add seasoning if desired then serve. Serves 4-6.

ROAST VENISON

small joint of venison
vinegar
water
9 peppercorns
2 bay leaves
sprig of rosemary
1 teaspoon thyme
1 teaspoon salt
6 bacon rashers
oil or dripping
1 glass red wine
½ cup sour cream
2 tablespoons redcurrant jelly

Marinate joint for 24-48 hours in a mixture of two parts vinegar to one part water plus peppercorns, bay leaves, rosemary, thyme and salt. Remove and wipe dry. Cover with rashers of bacon and place in a baking dish. Add generous amount of dripping or oil and roast in a hot oven, allowing 25 minutes per 500g. Baste frequently with pan juices and remove strips of bacon 20 minutes before meat is cooked, to allow joint to brown. When cooked, remove meat from roasting dish and keep warm. Drain off fat and add wine and sour cream to pan juices, blend thoroughly. Then stir in redcurrant jelly and pour sauce over meat. Serves 6-8.

SKEWERED VENISON STEAKS

875g-1kg good quality venison
  steak (about 3cm thick)
1 cup rosé or dry white wine (or 1
  cup regular strength beef broth)
2 tablespoons lemon juice
1 tablespoon honey
1 teaspoon seasoned salt
few drops Tabasco sauce
½ cup tomato sauce
1 spring onion, chopped

Cut steak across grain into diagonal strips about 12mm wide. Combine wine, lemon juice, honey, seasoned salt and Tabasco sauce. Pour over meat and marinate several hours or overnight. Drain meat well, saving marinade. Thread steak strips onto skewers, grill until rare or medium-rare. At the same time add tomato sauce to remaining drained marinade and heat to boiling. Spoon hot sauce over meat and sprinkle generously with chopped spring onion. Serves 6.
Note: For best flavour and texture, serve prime cuts of venison.

VENISON STEAK UREWERA

large loin of venison, about 600g
180g green bacon
olive oil
black pepper
salt
oil for cooking
50ml dry white wine
180ml cream
300ml demi-glace or game sauce
6 small peach halves
6 tablespoons kiwifruit purée
6 cocktail cherries

Bone saddle of venison and trim off all skin. Lard loin with strips of green bacon and cut into 6 equal portions. Pound gently, dip in olive oil, season with black pepper and salt and fry in very hot pan to medium-rare. Remove steaks, pour off excess fat, de-glace with a little of the white wine and the cream. Reduce and add demi-glace. Bring to boil and simmer.

Lay peach halves in casserole, pour white wine over, cover casserole and steam peaches until they are hot. Remove from casserole and fill peaches with kiwifruit purée. Garnish each half with cocktail cherry and arrange around venison steaks. Pour sauce over steaks. Serves 4-6.

Note: If no saddle is available a young haunch can be used. Meat must be well hung.

SALADS

CUCUMBER SALAD

650g large cucumbers, peeled and
    thinly sliced
salt
2 small onions
2 tablespoons lemon juice
2 teaspoons anchovy paste
2 tablespoons coconut milk
2 small chilli peppers, seeded, one
    shredded, one finely chopped

Sprinkle cucumber slices with salt and leave until soft. Toss slices lightly. Cut onions into thin slices, separating each ring. Soak in cold water and drain. Mix lemon juice with anchovy paste and add coconut milk and small amount of finely chopped chilli pepper. Mix in cucumbers and onions. Place in salad bowl and sprinkle with the shredded pepper. Serves 4-6.

CUCUMBER SALAD WITH CRAB

1 cucumber, unpeeled
salt
½ cup wine vinegar
240g crab or shrimp
½ teaspoon monosodium glutamate
1 cup oil
2 tablespoons soy sauce
½ teaspoon sugar
2 tablespoons dill leaves, chopped
fruit for garnish
1 hard-boiled egg

Slice the unpeeled cucumber, sprinkle with salt, allow to 'sweat' for 20 minutes and then drain. Sprinkle dry cucumber slices with vinegar then drain this juice well. Add crab or shrimps to the cucumber. Blend vinegar with a little salt, the glutamate, oil, soy sauce, sugar and dill leaves and pour over the salad arranged for serving. Garnish the top with fruit and hard-boiled egg slices. Serves 4-6.

CUCUMBER AND PINEAPPLE SALAD

pineapple chunks
1 cucumber
mayonnaise
1 lettuce
tomatoes

Drain pineapple chunks. Peel, seed and dice cucumber. Immediately before serving, combine with mayonnaise. Serve on a bed of lettuce or in tomato cups. Serves 4-6.

TURKEY SALAD

1 small can corn
¼ can small peas
½ cup mayonnaise
½ cup sour cream
1 pinch curry powder
1 pinch ginger powder
pinch saffron powder
salt and pepper
300g turkey meat, diced

Mix together corn and peas. Stir together mayonnaise, sour cream, curry powder, ginger, saffron and salt and pepper and bind in corn, peas and turkey. Allow salad to come up to room temperature before serving. Serves 4.

TAHITIAN SALAD

8 small beets
4 oranges, peeled (white membrane removed)
4 red apples, unpeeled but cored
4 bananas, peeled
1 fresh pineapple, peeled and cored, or 1 x 400g can pineapple chunks
3 limes, peeled (white membrane removed)
1 head lettuce
¼ cup sugar (optional)
seeds of 2 pomegranates
1 cup peanuts, chopped
1 cup tart French dressing or 1 cup orange juice

Thinly slice beets, oranges, apples, bananas, pineapple (if fresh) and limes. Shred lettuce. Put lettuce in bottom of a large shallow bowl and arrange fruits over it, sprinkling with the sugar if you choose to use it. Arrange the top layer attractively, perhaps with a ring of oranges around the outer edge, then beets, then pineapple in the centre. Sprinkle pomegranate seeds and chopped peanuts all over. Just before serving pour on the French dressing or the orange juice. Mix gently. Serves 6-8.

SALAD – BOSTON STYLE

5 potatoes
5 tomatoes
¼ celery heart
2 onions
1 cup wine vinegar
½ stalk celery
5 hard-boiled eggs, sliced
120g raw mushrooms, sliced
1 red pepper
1 green pepper

For dressing:
1 teaspoon salt
4 teaspoons oil
½ teaspoon mustard
2 hard-boiled egg yolks
2 tablespoons mayonnaise
2 tablespoons paprika
2 teaspoons sugar
white pepper

Boil potatoes in their jackets and allow to cool. Slash a cross into tomatoes and scald and skin them. Thickly peel celery heart and onions and cut into fine strips. Pour boiling wine vinegar over both and let soak for 5 minutes, then drain and cool. Save vinegar. Mix in celery stalk cut into strips, the eggs and raw mushrooms, and the red and green peppers sliced into rings. To make dressing, blend together salt, oil, mustard, egg yolks, mayonnaise, paprika, wine vinegar (drained from above), sugar and pepper. Blend well and marinate salad in dressing for 30 minutes. Serves 4-6.

LYCHEE ROAST CHICKEN SALAD

1 roasted chicken
2 teaspoons soy sauce
1 teaspoon sesame oil
1 can of lychees
parsley

Bone and shred the meat. Mix with soy sauce and sesame oil. Quarter lychees and sprinkle over chicken. Garnish with parsley. Serves 4-6.

SWEDISH SALAD

2 apples
2 boiled potatoes
2 pickled cucumbers
1 boiled carrot
2 tablespoons boiled celery heart
120g boiled ham
120g boiled brisket of beef
½ cup walnuts
300g ripe plums
2 tablespoons mayonnaise
3 tablespoons sour cream
juice of 1 lemon
1 head of lettuce

Peel and cube apples, potatoes, cucumbers, carrots and celery. Cube meat, chop walnuts, scald and skin plums and squeeze out the stones. Beat up mayonnaise, sour cream and lemon and blend all ingredients above. Serve on lettuce leaves. Serves 4-6.

SPANISH APPETISER SALAD

750g boiled new potatoes
1 large can tuna fish
12 black olives
12 green olives
2 hard-boiled eggs, sliced

For French dressing:
3 tablespoons wine vinegar
8-10 tablespoons olive oil
salt and pepper
dash of cayenne pepper

Peel and slice cold potatoes. Make dressing by blending together ingredients. A quarter teaspoon of each of the following adds much to this simple dressing: poppy seed, sesame seed and celery seed. Toss potatoes lightly in dressing and arrange in a shallow salad bowl. Drain tuna fish, break fish into chunks and place on top of potatoes. Garnish dish with black and green olives and sliced hard-boiled eggs, pour over remaining French dressing and serve immediately. Serves 4-6.

CHICKEN TOSS SALAD

1 cup cooked and shredded chicken
  breast
1 cup ham, shredded
1 cup abalone, shredded
1 small cucumber, skinned and
  diced
shredded lettuce
4 teaspoons vinegar
3 tablespoons sugar
1 teaspoon salt
1 teaspoon sesame oil
parsley

Mix chicken, ham, abalone, cucumber and lettuce together. Mix other ingredients together, pour over the chicken mixture and lightly toss. Garnish with parsley. Serves 4-6.

CHICKEN SALAD À LA KAI-TAK

100g celery, sliced
100g bean sprouts
230g cooked roast chicken, diced
4 soupspoons dry sherry
tomato halves, cut into rosettes
1 big carrot, grated

For dressing:
10g sugar
2 soupspoons sesame oil
2 soupspoons peanut oil
6 soupspoons soy sauce
1 teaspoon fresh ginger juice
100ml wine vinegar
salt and pepper

Blanch celery and bean sprouts very quickly (keep them crisp), then make up the dressing. Marinate chicken in sherry for 3 hours. Mix in celery and bean sprouts and stuff into half tomatoes. Garnish with grated carrot. Five tomatoes make 10 portions.

INDIAN CHICKEN SALAD

120g mayonnaise
1 teaspoon curry powder
1 teaspoon paprika
½ clove garlic
salt and pepper
120g ham, diced
360g chicken, diced
120g pineapple, diced
120g apples, diced

Season mayonnaise with equal parts of curry and paprika and a little garlic very finely crushed. Season to taste and mix into meats and fruits. Serves 4-6.

VEGETABLE AND CHICKEN SALAD APIA STYLE

80g snow-peas
250g potatoes, cut into shoestrings
2 chicken wings
3 small red chilli peppers, finely chopped
4 small onions, finely chopped
1 clove garlic, finely chopped
3 tablespoons coconut oil or salad oil
½ cup peanuts, skinned and crushed
¾ cup coconut milk
salt
2-3 tablespoons lime juice
700g cucumbers, shredded in 4cm lengths
300g cabbage, shredded in 4cm lengths

Boil snow-peas in salted water then plunge into cold water and cut into thin, diagonal slices. Parboil potatoes in salted water taking care not to overcook – potato slices must retain their shape. Drain. Skin, bone and shred chicken wings. Salt the meat and boil. Mix together chilli peppers, onions, garlic and sauté over a medium heat in coconut oil in a small saucepan. Add peanuts, then slowly thin the mixture with coconut milk, adding a little at a time. Salt and allow to cool. Pour in lime juice (the final taste should be slightly acid). Mix in the shredded cucumbers and cabbage, the cooked peas, potatoes and chicken meat. Serves 4-6.

PRAWN SALAD

3-4 cups prawns
1 lettuce
lemon slices

For cocktail sauce:
2 tablespoons tomato sauce
1 tablespoon Worcestershire
 sauce
1 tablespoon white vinegar
few drops Tabasco sauce
pinch of salt
½ teaspoon mustard
2 tablespoons cream, lightly
 whipped

Shell prawns, reserving 6 large ones for garnish. Shred lettuce and arrange layer of lettuce in each serving dish. Make sauce by combining all ingredients, except whipped cream, and mixing well. Fold in whipped cream. Place prawns on lettuce beds, spoon over cocktail sauce and garnish the side of each dish with lemon slices and reserved prawns. Serves 4-6.

NORWEGIAN SALAD

250g cod, perch or haddock, boiled
 and drained
2 pickled cucumbers
30g peas
120g carrots
1 apple, grated
1 orange, cubed
1 head lettuce
1 cup of lobster pieces

For dressing:
2 tablespoons oil
2 tablespoons wine vinegar
3 tablespoons water
3 tablespoons sugar
½ teaspoon salt
dash of paprika
dash of pepper

Pull boiled, drained pieces of fish into bite-sized pieces. Remove bones. Place in bowl and mix in chopped pickled cucumbers, peas, carrots, apple and cubed orange. Line salad bowl with lettuce leaves and carefully transfer fish mixture into it. Pour on salad dressing and garnish with lobster. Place in refrigerator for 30 minutes. Serve with buttered toast. Serves 4-6.

HERRING SALAD

4 white herring fillets
1 cup pickled red beets
1 pickled cucumber
2 apples
5 boiled potatoes
5 tablespoons wine vinegar
¼ teaspoon pepper
1 tablespoon onion, cubed
1 hard-boiled egg
1 bunch parsley
4 anchovy fillets
1 cup sour cream

Remove skin and bones from herring fillets; wash and cut into chunky pieces. Chop red beets, pickled cucumber and apples into chunky pieces. Peel and cube boiled potatoes and mix while still warm with mixture of vinegar, pepper and onion (the potatoes absorb the acid of the dressing more easily when warm). Cool for 30 minutes in refrigerator. Decorate with chopped egg and parsley and anchovy fillets. Serve with sour cream. Serves 4-6.

MACKEREL SALAD

3 x 200g cans mackerel
1 large can mandarin segments
2 sticks celery
3 tablespoons white wine
1 teaspoon soy sauce
juice of 1 lemon
salt and pepper
1 lettuce

Strain half the oil from the fish and break fish up into small pieces. Drain mandarins well. Clean and slice celery, saving a few leaves for garnish. For the sauce, mix together white wine, soy sauce and lemon juice. Season. Mix two-thirds of sauce with fish and mandarin. Mix remaining sauce with shredded lettuce. Place lettuce in the bottom of a salad bowl and fill with fish-mandarin mixture. Garnish with celery leaves. Serves 4-6.

TAHITIAN FISH SALAD

500g white fish (snapper or mullet)
salt
½ cup lemon or lime juice
½ onion, finely chopped
1 carrot, grated
1 small cucumber, diced
1 small green pepper, chopped
2 tomatoes, sliced
1 cup cabbage, shredded
½ cup French dressing
lettuce leaves

Cut fish into 1cm cubes. Sprinkle with salt, place in a bowl and cover with ½ cup lemon or lime juice. Leave for 2 hours or until white. Strain and squeeze out the juice by pressing in a strainer. Combine fish with salad vegetables and toss well in French dressing. Serve heaped on lettuce leaves. Serves 4-6.

COCONUT SEA SALAD

1 coconut
1-2kg fillets of sea bass, groper or
   ocean perch, diced
2 tablespoons coarse salt
juice of 2 lemons
1 onion, minced
1 hard-boiled egg, chopped fine
¼ teaspoon freshly ground black
   pepper
2 lemons, quartered

Crack open coconut, reserve the milk and grate white meat very fine. Place the fish in a deep bowl and sprinkle with coarse salt. Marinate in the salt for 2 hours. Remove fish, sponge off the salt carefully with a clean cloth and dry fish thoroughly. Place fish in the middle of a deep serving dish. Combine lemon juice, onion, grated coconut meat, coconut milk, the egg and pepper and pour the mixture over the fish. Toss lightly, arrange lemon quarters on top of the fish and chill. Set the dish into another filled with cracked ice when serving. Serves 6.

THAI CRAYFISH SALAD

120g unsalted coconut, shredded
2 cups milk
2 crayfish
salt
bay leaf
10 cloves
1 teaspoon sugar
fruit for garnish

For dressing:
8 shallots, sliced
2 cloves garlic, sliced
2 tablespoons oil
1 apple, grated
1 tablespoon soy sauce
1 knife-tip ground pepper
salt
1 green pepper, minced
5 tablespoons peanuts, grated
2 heads lettuce

Bring shredded coconut to a boil in milk, allow to stand for 30 minutes then squeeze out coconut in a cloth. (You need only the milk and can use the dry shredded coconut for cakes or something similar.) Bring crayfish to a boil with water, salt, bay leaf, cloves and sugar, then remove the pot from heat and stand for 10 minutes. Remove crayfish, split them in half lengthways and place in a cool place.

In the meantime, prepare dressing by tossing shallot and garlic slices in oil, then cooling. Mix with grated apple, soy sauce, pepper, salt, green pepper, peanuts and cold coconut milk. The dressing must be uniform and creamy in consistency. Add prepared crayfish tails and blend thoroughly. Arrange mixture on lettuce hearts and garnish with fruit. Chill before serving. Serves 4.

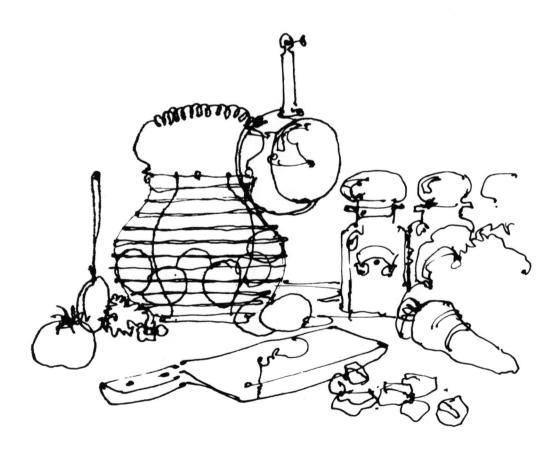

VEGETABLES

GLAZED TURNIPS

800g turnips
50g butter
2 tablespoons sugar
½ cup bouillon or gravy if desired
salt and pepper

Clean and slice turnips. Melt butter in a pot to cover the bottom and, stirring vigorously, lightly brown sugar in this. Add turnip slices and brown them on all sides until glazed. Pour on bouillon, sprinkle with salt and pepper to taste and let simmer briefly over a low heat. The bouillon may then be poured off and allowed to cook in another pot until it begins to thicken, or else it can be thickened with a little gravy. Serves 4-6.

LYONNAISE CARROTS

2 small onions, chopped
¼ cup butter
½ teaspoon salt
¼ teaspoon pepper
4 cups cooked carrots
1 tablespoon parsley, chopped

Brown onions in butter and add salt, pepper and carrots. Cover and cook slowly for about 15 minutes. Sprinkle with parsley. Serves 6-8.

COURGETTES SPANISH STYLE

8-12 courgettes
salt
flour
freshly ground black pepper
freshly grated Parmesan cheese
olive oil
chopped fresh tomatoes
1 onion

Boil courgettes in salted water until just tender – do not let them lose their shape. Cut into thick slices, dust with seasoned flour then roll in Parmesan cheese. Fry in hot oil until golden brown on both sides. Place on kitchen paper to remove excess fat and serve hot with chopped fresh tomatoes.

To prepare tomatoes, peel 6 tomatoes in the following manner: place tomatoes on the end of a kitchen fork and hold in boiling water for a minute or two (until skin begins to crack). With a sharp knife gently peel off skin. Cut tomatoes in half and remove seeds, then chop roughly into cubes. Dice onion, season with salt and freshly ground black pepper and combine with chopped tomatoes. Simmer gently in butter until onion is cooked through. Serves 4-6.

STUFFED TOMATOES

8 small tomatoes (not too ripe)
pinch of salt
18 anchovies, chopped
1 medium-sized can tuna
18 capers, crushed
3 tablespoons mayonnaise
1 tablespoon parsley, chopped
3 eggs, hard-boiled

Wash tomatoes and dry. Cut in half, scoop out seeds and sprinkle with salt. Chill in refrigerator for 30 minutes. Blend anchovies, tuna and capers with mayonnaise. Fill each tomato half with the mixture, sprinkle with parsley and garnish with sliced eggs. Serves 4.

SPANISH STUFFED ONIONS

4-6 large onions
olive oil
2 level tablespoons breadcrumbs

For stuffing
1 chopped, sautéed onion
2 slices white bread, soaked in
   water, squeezed dry and shredded
115g veal or beef, chopped
1 egg yolk
olive oil
1-2 tablespoons parsley, chopped
1-2 cups spinach, chopped
butter
½ level teaspoon salt
¼ level teaspoon freshly ground
   black pepper

Peel onions and cut in halves crossways. Boil in water for 8 minutes. Cool by placing in cold water for a few minutes then drain well. Remove 3 or 4 layers from centre of each onion half to make room for stuffing. Chop these pieces coarsely and sauté in 2 tablespoons olive oil until soft.

For the stuffing, combine chopped, sautéed onion (above) with shredded bread, chopped veal or beef, egg yolk, 2 tablespoons olive oil, chopped parsley and chopped spinach which you have simmered in a little butter. Mix well, add salt and pepper and stuff onion halves with this mixture. Place stuffed onions in a well-greased baking dish; sprinkle with breadcrumbs and 2 tablespoons olive oil, and bake in a moderate oven (190°C) for 1 hour. Serves 4-6.

BAKED PEPPERS ITALIENNE

4 large green peppers
olive oil
170g toasted breadcrumbs
3 level tablespoons seedless raisins
12 black olives, pitted and cut into
   pieces
2 tablespoons parsley, chopped
6 anchovy fillets, cut into small
   pieces
1 tablespoon fresh basil or tarragon,
   chopped
2 tablespoons capers, chopped
salt and freshly ground black pepper
4 tablespoons tomato sauce
anchovy fillets for garnish

Wash peppers thoroughly. Cut through stem ends of peppers and scoop out seeds and fibres. Combine 6 to 8 tablespoons olive oil, breadcrumbs, raisins, olives, chopped parsley, anchovies, basil and capers in a large mixing bowl. Add salt and freshly ground black pepper to taste and mix well. Add a little more oil if necessary. Stuff peppers with mixture and place in a heatproof baking dish which you have brushed with olive oil. Sprinkle peppers with olive oil and top each one with 1 tablespoon tomato sauce. Bake in a moderate oven (190°C) for 1 hour. Garnish with anchovy fillets and tomato sauce. Excellent hot or cold. Serves 4.

STUFFED CHINESE MARROW OR PAW PAW

Chinese marrow or medium paw
   paw
1 cup cooked, seasoned
   mincemeat
¾ cup cooked rice
1 small onion, finely chopped
2 tablespoons oil
2 tablespoons parsley, chopped
1 egg, beaten
1 teaspoon salt
pepper to taste
pinch of sugar

Cut off end of marrow and set aside or remove stalk end of paw paw and save this. Remove seeds with a spoon. Mix cooked meat with cooked rice. Fry onion in oil and mix in bowl with parsley, marrow, meat, rice and sugar. Stir in egg, season with salt and pepper. Mix everything very well and stuff into paw paw or marrow. Fix cut end in place with a toothpick. Brush with oil or melted butter and bake at 180°C until soft. Serve with tomato sauce or gravy. Serves 2.

Overleaf:
Bonadventure Hotel, Los Angeles

Pavlova with Fresh Cream and Fruit,
Tasty Toheroa Special and Leg of Lamb Aotearoa

BROCCOLI FLORENTINE

1 large trimmed bunch broccoli
1 clove garlic, crushed
¼ cup olive or salad oil
salt and pepper
generous sprinkling of Parmesan
cheese

Boil broccoli until barely done then drain. Heat garlic in frying pan with the oil, then add broccoli and sauté until tender, turning occasionally. Season with salt, pepper and cheese. Serves 4-6.

SPINACH WITH HARD-BOILED EGGS AND PIMENTO

1kg fresh spinach
4 tablespoons olive oil
salt and freshly ground black pepper
1 clove garlic, finely chopped
2 hard-boiled eggs, sliced
1 can or 2 fresh pimentos

Wash spinach leaves in several changes of water and drain. Place spinach in a thick-bottomed saucepan with olive oil, season to taste with salt and pepper and a very little finely chopped garlic, and cook over medium heat, stirring constantly, until spinach is soft and melted. Transfer spinach to a heated serving dish. Top with slices of hard-boiled egg and strips of pimento. Serves 4.

BLUE-CHEESED TOMATOES

8 tomatoes, sliced
2 spring onions, sliced
sprigs of parsley
1 lettuce
90g cream cheese
½ cup crumbled blue vein cheese
½ cup mayonnaise
½ cup evaporated milk
1 tablespoon lemon juice

Arrange some of the sliced tomatoes and all the spring onions and parsley on a bed of lettuce. Soften cream cheese and blend in blue vein cheese. Gradually add mayonnaise, evaporated milk and lemon juice. Chill. Top with tomato slices and serve. Serves 4.

GREEN BEANS WITH CHEESE

4 cups cooked green beans
¼ teaspoon salt
⅛ teaspoon cayenne pepper
¾ cup grated cheese
2 tablespoons butter
⅓ cup cream

Arrange beans in a greased baking dish and season with salt and cayenne. Add ½ cup of the cheese, 1 tablespoon butter and cream and stir until well mixed. Sprinkle with remaining cheese and dot with remaining butter. Bake in a hot oven at 205°C for about 20 minutes. Serves 6.

CABBAGE AND CELERY CASSEROLE

½ cup celery, chopped
5 tablespoons butter
3½ cups cabbage, chopped
½ teaspoon salt
⅛ teaspoon pepper
1 cup white sauce
1 tablespoon green pepper, chopped
¼ cup dry breadcrumbs

Cook celery in 3 tablespoons butter, stirring frequently. Add cabbage and cook for 10 minutes longer. Pour into greased baking dish, add salt, pepper, white sauce and green pepper. Sprinkle breadcrumbs over the top, dot with remaining butter and bake in a moderate oven at 175°C for about 20 minutes. Serves 6.

Previous page: Venison Steak Urewera, Avocado with Ravigote Mayonnaise and Strawberries Romanoff

Regent Hotel, Nadi, Fiji

99

LITTLE WHITE BEANS À LA BRETON

500g small white beans
salt and pepper
1 piece (100g) bacon
1 clove garlic
thyme ⎫
bay leaf ⎬ bouquet garni
parsley ⎭
3-4 cloves
3 onions
40g butter
1 tablespoon tomato paste

Soak beans overnight in a cooking pot. Just before cooking add salt and pepper, bacon, garlic and the thyme, bay leaf and parsley tied together. Press cloves into one of the onions and add. Bring to the boil and simmer gently. Chop remaining onions and fry lightly in butter until transparent. Add tomato paste and season with salt and pepper and some of the cooking liquid from the beans. Strain beans, removing all seasoning, and add to onion-tomato paste mixture. Mix well. Chop bacon and add to sauce. Serve with lamb cutlets. Serves 4-6.

PEAS WITH EGG SAUCE

500g shelled peas or 1 large packet
    frozen peas
salt
4 hard-boiled egg yolks
1 boiled potato
1¼-1¾ cups olive oil
1-2 teaspoons wine vinegar
freshly ground black pepper
2 tablespoons parsley, finely
    chopped
2 tablespoons hard-boiled egg
    whites, finely chopped

Cook peas until tender in boiling salted water. Pound egg yolks and boiled potato to a paste in a mortar (or press through a fine sieve). Beat in olive oil and vinegar until smooth. Season to taste with salt and freshly ground black pepper. Drain peas and mix with sauce. Sprinkle with parsley and the hard-boiled egg whites. Serves 4-6.

CHINESE VEGETABLES BUDDHIST STYLE

115g dried oysters, soaked in water
    for 2 hours
115g hearts of Chinese cabbage
115g dried bean curd strips, soaked
    in water for 1 hour
115g fried bean curd
115g can bamboo shoots
60g Chinese black mushrooms,
    soaked in water for 30 minutes
115g snow pea pods, peeled
115g fat choy (dried seaweed)
115g rice noodles
60g Chinese white ginkgo nuts
4 cups chicken broth
2 teaspoons salt
1 tablespoon sugar
¼ cup oyster sauce
2 cakes of foo yoo (Chinese cheese)

Clean oysters thoroughly in several rinsings of water. Place oysters, cleaned vegetables, noodles and nuts into a saucepan with chicken broth. Cook for 15 minutes, stirring in salt, sugar, and oyster sauce gradually. Add 2 cakes of foo yoo and simmer for 30 minutes. Serves 4-6.

VEGETABLES IN COCONUT GRAVY

500-750g mixed vegetables
2 tablespoons peanut oil
1 onion, finely chopped
2 cloves garlic, crushed
1 teaspoon sambal ulek, or 1 fresh
 red chilli, seeded and chopped
1 teaspoon trasi (dried shrimp paste)
1 stalk lemon grass, or 2 strips
 lemon rind, or ½ teaspoon sereh
 powder
1 large ripe tomato, peeled, seeded
 and chopped
2 cups vegetable, chicken or beef
 stock
1½ cups coconut milk
3 teaspoons peanut sauce or peanut
 butter
2 teaspoons salt, or to taste

Slice vegetables into small pieces; cauliflower or broccoli should be broken or cut into flowerets; beans sliced very thinly; cabbage shredded coarsley and the shreds cut across once or twice – if they are too long it makes the dish awkward to eat; zucchini or pumpkin can be sliced thinly or diced and winter bamboo shoots, much more tender than the ordinary variety, cut into short strips, or they can be halved and sliced for a half-moon shape.

Heat oil in a medium saucepan and fry onion until soft and starting to colour, then add garlic, sambal and trasi and fry over a low heat for 2 minutes, crushing the trasi with back of spoon and stirring the mixture. Add lemon grass or substitute and the tomato. Stir and cook to a pulp. Add stock and coconut milk and bring to simmering point with lid off. Add vegetables according to the time they take to cook. They should be cooked tender but still crisp. In the selection above you would add the beans, simmer for 4 minutes, then add cauliflower and broccoli, simmer for a further 3 minutes, then cabbage, zucchini, pumpkin and bamboo shoots and cook for 3 minutes longer. Stir in peanut sauce and add salt to taste. A squeeze of lemon juice may be added if a sharper flavour is preferred. Serves 4-6.

VEGETABLE PULAO

230g patna or basmati rice
oil for frying
4 cloves
2 whole cardamom seeds
1 teaspoon whole cumin or caraway
 seeds
2 sticks cinnamon
2 onions, sliced
4 carrots, sliced into rounds
170g shelled peas
2½ cups chicken stock or water
salt to taste

Wash rice well and leave aside with enough water to cover. Heat a little oil in a heavy saucepan and fry cloves, cardamom and cumin seeds and cinnamon for a minute. Add onions, carrots and peas and fry for another 5 minutes. Pour in stock, season with salt and cook uncovered for 15 minutes. Remove, cover and finish cooking in a moderate oven (180°C) for another 15 minutes. Serves 4-6.

SAUERKRAUT DISH

100g smoky bacon, diced
butter
1 onion, finely chopped
1kg sauerkraut
1 stock cube dissolved in 350ml
 water
1 handful seedless raisins
1kg potatoes, boiled
1-2 smoked sausages
milk
2 tomatoes, sliced
grated cheese

Cook diced bacon slowly in a little butter together with the onion. Add three-quarters of the sauerkraut, stirring constantly, then stock and raisins and allow to cook slowly for 30 minutes. Boil potatoes. Warm the smoked sausage in water (do not boil). Mash potatoes with milk and butter. Butter an oven dish and add layer upon layer – cooked sauerkraut mixed with the finely chopped remainder of the raw sauerkraut, and mashed potato. Slice smoked sausage and place pieces on top of mashed potato (like roof tiles) together with pieces of tomato. Sprinkle with grated cheese and place in a warm oven (175°C) until cooked through. Serves 4-6.

DESSERTS

PAVLOVA WITH FRESH CREAM AND FRUIT

4 egg whites
pinch of citric acid
60g castor sugar
14g cornflour
whipped cream
fruit

In a double-boiler, hand-whisk together egg whites, citric acid and castor sugar until hot. Remove from double-boiler and beat until meringue 'peaks'. Fold in cornflour by hand. Turn out meringue in discs on trays covered with greaseproof paper. Build up sides of discs. Bake at 100°C until outsides of pavlovas turn hard then reduce to 50°C, for 1½ hours. When cool fill in middle of pavlovas with fresh whipped cream and decorate with fresh fruit. Makes 2 pavlovas.

CARAMEL APPLES

6 apples
45g flour
15g cornflour
2 egg whites
oil for deep frying
½ cup granulated sugar
1 tablespoon oil
1 tablespoon sesame seeds

Peel, core and quarter apples and dust them lightly with some of the plain flour. Sift remaining flour with cornflour into a bowl. Add egg whites and mix to a paste. Deep fry in hot oil until golden. Drain well. Place sugar in saucepan with 2 tablespoons water. Heat, stirring constantly, until sugar is dissolved. Add oil and continue heating slowly until sugar caramelises and is a light golden brown. Stir in the apple and sesame seeds. Serve immediately in lightly oiled dishes. Place a bowl of cold water on the table so guests may drop the apple in the water to harden the caramel before eating. Serves 6.

BANANAS WITH CREAM

5-7 ripe bananas
lemon juice
4 tablespoons butter
8 tablespoons sherry
brown sugar
1¼ cups cream
½ teaspoon vanilla essence
1 small jar sour or maraschino
  cherries

Peel 4 bananas and slice in half lengthways. Brush banana halves with lemon juice to preserve their colour. Melt 1 tablespoon butter in each of 4 individual oval baking dishes; place bananas flat-side up in dishes, (2 halves to each dish) and sauté gently in oven until golden. Turn banana halves and sauté other sides. Remove from heat, sprinkle with sherry and a little brown sugar. Whip cream, add vanilla essence. Decorate bananas with cream. Peel remaining bananas and cut into slices, brush with lemon juice. Garnish each dish with a few slices of banana and a few cherries. Sprinkle with brown sugar. Serves 4.

CREAMY KIWIFRUIT SHERBET

1¼ cups sugar
2 teaspoons lemon peel, grated
4 soft kiwifruit, peeled
pinch of salt
2 cups cream
few drops of green colouring
whipped cream
chocolate decoration

Chill egg-beater and large bowl in refrigerator. In another bowl blend together sugar, lemon peel, kiwifruit, salt, cream and colouring. Pour into a flat tray and freeze. When frozen turn mixture into the chilled bowl and beat with chilled beater until smooth but not melted. Place in long-stemmed glasses and freeze until firm. Garnish with whipped cream rosettes and chocolate diamonds. Serves 10-12.

GOOSEBERRY LATTICE PIE

500g gooseberries
150ml water
180g sugar
30g cornflour
1 teaspoon cinnamon
1 teaspoon cloves
grated nutmeg
short pastry
30g butter

Top and tail fruit and cook with the water and 120g sugar. Mix rest of the sugar, cornflour and spices. When fruit is tender, add cornflour-spice mixture and cook, stirring, until thick. Line pie plate (25-30cm) with rolled out pastry, crimp the edges. Fill with fruit mixture and dot with butter. Cover with strips of pastry arranged in a lattice pattern and bake in a moderate oven for about 30 minutes. Serve with whipped cream or custard. Serves 10-12.

MANDARIN CREAM TART

7g gelatin
15g cornflour
300ml milk
2 eggs
150g castor sugar
grated rind of 1 lemon
150ml whipped cream
1 can mandarin oranges
1 baked sweet short-pastry shell

Dissolve gelatin in a little water. Blend cornflour with a little milk and heat remainder. Pour hot milk onto cornflour, return to pan and cook for several minutes. Remove from heat and add egg yolks, 30g castor sugar, gelatin and lemon rind. Cool, then fold in cream. Arrange most of the mandarin segments on pastry shell, spoon over cream and leave to set. Beat egg whites with remainder of sugar until stiff. Pile meringue onto pie and bake at 205°C until crisp. Decorate with remaining mandarin segments. Serves 8-10.

OPEN FRUIT FLAN

(Basic method for all open flans where filling need not be cooked.)

500g sweet pastry

For filling:
apricot purée
fruit
1 teaspoon gelatin

Line 23cm flan tin with sweet pastry approximately 3mm thick. Bake blind in oven at 180°C until pastry is set and firm. Remove paper and rice and replace in oven. Bake to a golden brown.

Brush bottom of flan case with apricot purée to prevent the juice of any fruit being used, making the pastry soggy. Having placed the fruit of your choice in the flan case make a glaze by dissolving gelatin in sufficient boiling water (about ½ cup). If tinned fruit is being used for fruit filling, the juice from fruit may be added to gelatin for the glaze. Otherwise make up a sugar syrup by dissolving 8 tablespoons castor sugar in boiling water. Glaze top of flan, ensuring that all fruit is properly covered, and allowed to set. Flans may be garnished with fresh cream if desired. Serves 6-8.

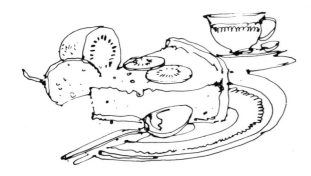

TAMARILLO FLAN

2 cups flour
2 tablespoons sugar
1 teaspoon baking powder
pinch of salt
120g butter
1 egg
1kg tamarillos
¾ cup sugar
1 cup water
1 tablespoon cornflour
1 tablespoon butter

Sift flour, 2 tablespoons sugar, baking powder and salt, rub in butter. Add egg and work to a paste. Grease a large pie dish and line with mixture. Prick bottom and bake at 190°C until golden. Scald and peel tamarillos, stew in sugar and water until tender, drain. Mix cornflour with cold water and stir into syrup with butter and a dash of salt. Stir until thick, smooth and clear. Arrange fruit in case and spoon cooled glaze over. Chill and serve with whipped cream. Serves 6-8.

ITALIANNE BRANDIED FIGS

¼ teaspoon ground cinnamon
1 tablespoon orange rind, grated
2-4 tablespoons brandy
4 tablespoons sherry
8-12 fresh figs, or 1 large can figs, drained
icing sugar if desired
whipped cream
1-2 tablespoons toasted almonds

Combine cinnamon, grated orange rind, brandy and sherry and sprinkle over figs, with a little icing sugar if desired. Marinate figs in this flavouring for at least 1 hour before serving. Spoon whipped cream onto figs and garnish with toasted almonds. Serves 4.

LIME SOUFFLÉ

250ml white wine
250ml lime juice
8 eggs, separated
360g sugar
4 leaves gelatin or 25g powdered gelatin
250ml cream, whipped very stiff

Combine 200ml wine, lime juice, egg yolks and half the sugar. Heat in double-boiler until quite thick and foamy (do not boil). Take off heat, set basin in iced water and beat a few minutes more. Leave to cool. Dissolve gelatin in 50ml boiling wine and add to lime juice-egg mixture. Carefully fold in whipped cream. Beat egg whites with other half of sugar (180g) until very stiff, like meringue. Fold into mix, then fill cocktail glass. Chill and garnish. Alternatively, fill hollowed-out lemons. Serves 18-20.

ORANGE MOUSSE

orange jelly
2 oranges
1 lemon
4 eggs, separated
115g castor sugar
60g gelatin
1¼ cups cream, whipped

Make up orange jelly and set a little into bottom of mould. Grate orange rind into basin. Juice oranges and lemon and strain juice. Add to double-boiler with egg yolks and sugar and whisk until mixture is hot but not boiling. Dissolve gelatin in a little warm water, leave to cool, then add whipped cream and beaten egg whites. Pour into mould and chill in refrigerator. Serves 6-8.

ORANGE GIVRE

oranges
ice-cream
whipped cream

Cut top off oranges and remove flesh but don't damage skins. Fill with orange ice-cream, garnish with whipped cream, replace tops on oranges and keep in freezer until served.

Variation:
Soften ice-cream, add a shot of Grand Marnier and some whipped cream and mix well. Pipe into orange shells, refreeze and serve.

ORANGE DESSERT SPANISH STYLE

5 eggs, well beaten
2-3 tablespoons sugar
½ cup orange juice
juice of ½ lemon
½ teaspoon vanilla essence
   (optional)
½ cup milk
grated rind of ½ large orange
grated rind of ½ lemon
powdered cinnamon
chopped dates
sugar

Beat eggs and 2-3 tablespoons sugar until smooth then gradually beat in orange and lemon juice. Add vanilla essence if desired. Bring milk and grated orange and lemon rinds to a boil then beat into egg mixture. Pour into individual custard cups and sprinkle with powdered cinnamon. Fill a roasting pan half full of water. Place on top of the stove and allow water to come to a boil. Place filled custard cups carefully into water, ensuring water in pan does not come over the top of cups. Transfer pan to a pre-heated cool oven (160°C) and bake for 45 minutes, or until a silver knife inserted in centre of custards comes out clean. Just before serving top custards with chopped dates rolled in a little cinnamon and sugar. Serves 4-6.

STRAWBERRIES ROMANOFF

250g strawberries
shot brandy
180ml red wine
30g sugar
small pinch mixed spice
¼ vanilla stick
juice of ¼ lemon
red food colouring
2 egg whites
2 teaspoons sugar
180ml cream, partially whipped

Clean and hull strawberries. Soak half the strawberries overnight in brandy. Place remaining strawberries in long glasses. Make up mixture of red wine, sugar, mixed spice, vanilla stick and lemon juice. Bring to the boil, strain then allow to cool. Add a touch of colouring then pour into glasses just covering strawberries. Pulp soaked strawberries and sieve. Make meringue with egg whites and 2 tablespoons sugar, fold in pulp carefully and add partly whipped cream. This mixture is then piped over the strawberries in the glasses. Serves 4-6.

PINEAPPLE MELBA

½ cup strawberry jam
8 slices pineapple
4 cups ice cream
1 cup cream

Strain jam and chill. On each chilled plate place 1 slice of pineapple and top with ½ cup ice cream. Top again with cream and strawberry jam. Serve cold. Serves 8.

PISTACHIO PARFAIT

60g green pistachio nuts
2 or 3 tablespoons water
a few drops of kirsch
1 cup stock syrup at 32 degrees
8 egg yolks
ice
1¾ cups whipped cream

To make stock syrup: bring 1 cup of sugar and one cup of water to boil, take off heat.
Pound nuts with 2 or 3 tablespoons water and kirsch into a fine paste. Blend egg yolks into cold syrup. Beat up the mixture in a double-boiler over a gentle heat until it thickens. When it has well risen, remove mixture from double-boiler and place on ice, continuing to beat until mixture is completely cold. Add nut paste and whipped cream, pour into a mould and freeze for 2 hours. Serves 6-8.

LYCHEES AND MANDARINS

1 can lychees
1 can mandarin pieces
24 small ice cubes

Chop up lychees and mandarins and chill in the lychee juice. Add ice cubes and serve. Serves 6-8.

ALMOND LAKE AND PINEAPPLE

2½ cups milk
4 tablespoons sugar
1 teaspoon almond essence
60g ground rice
1 can sliced pineapple
30g flaked almond

Place milk in pan with sugar, almond essence and rice. Bring to boil and simmer for a few minutes, stirring all the time, then pour onto dish, cover, and cool. Drain pineapple, keeping the juice. Cut sliced pineapple in half and place pieces on top of the rice dish. Sprinkle with flaked almond. Pineapple juice may be used as a syrup as required. Serves 6-8.

LYCHEE PIE

230g sweet pastry
500g lychees
1 packet banana jelly
2 tablespoons gelatin
½ cup water
½ cup milk
juice of ½ lemon
60g sugar
½ cup cream

Roll out pastry and line a pie dish. Cover top with grease-proof paper, fill with rice and bake blind for 20 minutes, them remove paper and rice and bake for another 5 minutes. Shell and seed lychees if necessary. Set aside 5 lychees for decoration, chop up rest. Dissolve gelatin and jelly in the milk and water. Boil slowly then add lemon juice, sugar and lychee pieces. Mix together and leave to cool. Beat cream and add to the cool mixture. Pour mixture into pie and decorate with whole lychees. Serve chilled. Serves 10-12.

FRIED FEVIS PUFF

½ cup pitted dates
½ cup raisins
¼ cup dried apricots
¼ teaspoon salt
1 teaspoon sugar
margarine
1 teaspoon sesame seeds
2 eggs
½ cup cornflour
red food colouring
fat or butter

Chop dates, raisins and apricots together. Mix salt, sugar, margarine and sesame seeds together and make a batter using eggs, cornflour and a few drops of food colouring. Mix fruits into sesame seed-margarine mixture and mix well. Make 20-30 round balls out of the mixture and coat balls with batter. Deep fry in fat or lard till golden brown and remove. Drain and serve. Serves 10-12.

ALMOND BEAN CURD WITH PINEAPPLE, CHERRIES AND LYCHEES

1 envelope or 4 teaspoons of
  unflavoured gelatin
3 tablespoons cold water
½ cup evaporated milk
1½ cups water
3 tablespoons sugar
2 teaspoons almond extract
1 cup lychees with juice
⅓ cup maraschino cherries
½ cup pineapple chunks

Mix gelatin and cold water together in a saucepan. Place on low heat and stir until gelatin is dissolved. Add evaporated milk, water and sugar and stir until sugar is dissolved. Add almond extract. Pour mixture into 23 x 13 x 6cm dish and refrigerate. When set, cut into cubes, mix with lychees and juice, cherries and pineapple chunks and serve. Serves 8-10.

BAVAROIS À LA VANILLA

4 eggs
120g sugar
500ml milk
vanilla essence
30g gelatin
125ml cream, whipped
ice

Mix egg yolks and sugar and add heated milk and vanilla essence. Return to heat and thicken. Add dissolved gelatin. Strain and cool on ice until close to setting point, then fold through whipped cream and whipped egg whites and place into moulds. Serves 8-10.

BAVAROIS AU CHOCOLAT

As for standard recipe, adding 120g chocolate.

BAVAROIS AU CAFÉ

As for standard recipe adding coffee to the required strength.
Line bottom of mould with approx 1cm of coffee jelly.

ORANGE BAVAROIS

As for standard recipe, adding orange essence and a few drops
of orange colouring. Line bottom of mould with orange jelly
and arrange orange segments neatly around inside of mould.

CARAMEL PUDDING SINGAPORE STYLE

1½ cups sugar
2 tablespoons butter
4 tablespoons sugar
4 tablespoons flour
6 egg yolks
1¼ cups milk
2 tablespoons grated orange peel
1 heaped teaspoon vanilla sugar
1 small glass port
4 egg whites, stiffly beaten
½ cup raspberry jelly
½ cup cream

Melt and brown sugar in a small frying pan. Distribute resulting caramel equally into the bottoms of four cups. Beat butter until foamy, cream in sugar and flour until smooth then beat in egg yolks and stir mixture until fluffy. Add milk, grated orange peel, vanilla sugar, port and lastly, the egg whites. Pour this custard into the four cups and place on a baking sheet. Pour a little water onto the baking sheet and place in a preheated oven (250°C) for 20-25 minutes. After cooking turn out puddings and serve with a sauce made of raspberry jelly and cream. Preheat jelly, let cool and just before it sets fold cream in. Serves 4.

SPANISH CHOCOLATE PUDDING

115g cooking chocolate
250g butter, softened and diced
4 egg yolks
115g castor sugar
finely grated rind of 1 orange
12 tablespoons kirsch
lady fingers, boudoir biscuits or
   strips of stale sponge cake
1¼ cups cream, whipped

Melt chocolate and half the butter in a small saucepan. Remove from heat. Whisk egg yolks and sugar in the top of a double-boiler over hot water until thick and creamy. Stir melted chocolate into egg yolks, then stir in remaining butter. Beat until smooth. Add finely grated orange rind and kirsch. Butter a charlotte mould or a tall ice-cream bombe mould.
Mix remaining kirsch with an equal amount of water. Dip each lady finger, or substitute, in the mixture and place a layer of lady fingers in the bottom of the mould. Spoon a layer of chocolate mixture over the lady fingers, and continue with alternate layers of lady fingers and chocolate cream until the mould is filled, ending with a layer of lady fingers. Chill in the refrigerator overnight. When ready to serve, dip mould in a pan of very hot water for 2-3 minutes. Then unmould on to a serving dish. Serve with whipped cream. Serves 4-6.

MOUSSE AU CHOCOLAT

1 leaf gelatin or 6g powdered
   gelatin
45ml brandy
115g sweet chocolate powder
3 egg whites
25g sugar
250ml cream, whipped

Dissolve gelatin in a little warm water, add to lukewarm brandy and mix with chocolate powder. Set aside. Beat egg whites with sugar until very stiff. Fold chocolate mix into egg whites and then fold in whipped cream very carefully. (Don't beat or mix at this stage, use an over-and-under cutting motion). Turn out into glasses and chill. Decorate to your liking. Serves 4-6.

BLACK FOREST GATEAU

For cake:
100g butter
100g castor sugar
2 eggs
90g self-raising flour
15g cocoa
25g plain chocolate
1 tablespoon milk

For filling and decoration:
1 x 425g can pitted black cherries
2 level teaspoons cornflour
kirsch
3½ cups cream

Heat oven to 180°C and have ready a greased sandwich tin 23cm in diameter. Beat butter and sugar together until light and creamy then beat in the eggs one at a time. Sift flour and cocoa together and stir lightly into creamed mixture. Dissolve chocolate in warm milk, cool, then add to creamed mixture. Turn into prepared tin and bake in centre of oven for 25-30 minutes, or until springy to the touch. Turn out onto a wire rack to cool. Drain black cherries and pour 140ml of the syrup onto cornflour. Stir well. Turn into saucepan and bring to the boil, stirring all the time. Add drained cherries and leave to cool. Whisk cream until it begins to thicken. Have ready a serving plate. Split cake through the centre and place base on plate. Sprinkle with kirsch. Spread half whipped cream over sponge base and carefully spoon over most of the cherries in the syrup. Place other half of cake on top. Sprinkle with kirsch and decorate with the remaining cream and cherries. Serves 8-10.

GATEAU MEXICAN

130g sugar
1 egg yolk
4 eggs, separated
100g flour
37g cocoa
81g butter, melted
apricot jam
chocolate fondant
royal icing

Chocolate butter cream:
120g butter
90g icing sugar } cream together
30g cocoa powder

Whip sugar and five egg yolks to a stiff foam. Fold in stiffly whipped whites of four eggs and at the same time the flour and cocoa which have been sieved together. Fold in melted butter and pour into a ring or sandwich tin about 25cm in diameter. The tin should be greased and dusted lightly with flour. Bake in moderate oven (190°C) for 35-40 minutes. When baked and cold, slice through cake twice and sandwich with chocolate butter cream. Half fill with icing a small greaseproof paper piping-bag fitted with a small plain nozzle. Mask cake with well-boiled apricot jam and then with prepared chocolate fondant. Before the fondant has time to set, pipe parallel lines of icing across the top very quickly. Pass the point of a knife lightly over the top, first in one direction and then in the opposite direction to create a feathered effect. Serves 8-10.

SAVARIN

For dough:
280g flour
4 eggs
**1 tablespoon yeast (mixed in tepid
    milk)**
1½ teaspoons salt
1 tablespoon sugar
100g butter

For syrup:
500g sugar
1¼ cups water
orange and lemon zest
apricot purée
fruit
whipped cream
glace cherries

Hand mix dough ingredients together very well. Pipe savarin mix into greased ring moulds. Prove and then bake at 230°C. Savarins can be made the previous day in advance of requirements, or even kept in a deep freeze.
When required, make up a syrup with the sugar and water and bring to the boil. Add orange and lemon zest to flavour. Poach the savarins in the syrup. Remove from syrup and drain, glaze with apricot purée. The centre of savarins should be filled with a mixture of chopped soft fruits. Pipe around with fresh cream and garnish with glace cherries. Serves 10-12.

RUM BABAS

dough
sugar syrup
rum
whipped cream
cherries
angelica

Using the same dough recipe as for savarins (see above), fill some well greased patty moulds with the dough and allow to prove, bake at 230°C for 25-30 minutes. When cold these should be poached in a sugar syrup (again as for savarins) to which rum has been added. Then 'babas' may be split and fresh whipped cream piped in-between or left whole with rosette of fresh cream piped on top. Garnish each with a cherry and slice of angelica. Serves 10-12.

SCOTCH BUN (A CHRISTMAS SPECIAL)

115g butter
2 tablespoons sugar
3 eggs, beaten
1 cup flour
500g currants
30g almonds
1 teaspoon cinnamon
115g mixed peel
1 teaspoon allspice
½ teaspoon ginger, ground
500g raisins
¼ teaspoon cayenne pepper
1 teaspoon nutmeg
500g short pastry

Beat together butter and sugar, add most of the beaten eggs, then flour and all other ingredients except the short pastry. Line a cake tin with the pastry, place in mixture and cover with pastry top. Brush with beaten egg. Bake slowly at 150°C for 3 hours. Serves 20-25.

STOCKS, SAUCES AND DRESSINGS

CHICKEN STOCK

2.5kg chicken
400g veal bones
2 carrots, coarsely chopped
1 onion spiked with 3 cloves
6 peppercorns
2 teaspoons salt
1 stalk of celery, with leaves,
    coarsely cut
4 sprigs parsley
1 bay leaf
¼ teaspoon thyme
5*l* cold water

Put all ingredients into a large saucepan. Bring to the boil, reduce heat and simmer for 3 hours. Remove chicken (can use chicken for salad or other purposes). Boil the stock rapidly for 30 minutes then strain through a fine sieve. Cool and skim fat from the surface. Stock can be poured into containers and frozen, and used as required.
If quick chicken stock is required. Use 400ml water for 4 servings, and mix with commercial ready made chicken boullion to taste.

BEEF STOCK

80g beef shin, cubed
1.2kg veal knuckle, cubed
2 tablespoons cooking oil
3 carrots, sliced
2 onions, sliced
2 celery stalks
3 cloves garlic
4*l* cold water
parsley
½ teaspoon thyme
2 large bay leaves
2 teaspoons salt
1 teaspoon peppercorns, crushed

Preheat oven to 220°C. Place beef shin and veal knuckle in roasting pan, sprinkle with cooking oil and bake in very hot oven 45 minutes, stirring occasionally. Add carrots, onion, celery and garlic and bake further 15 minutes. Transfer meat and vegetables to a large saucepan, including all the cooking juices from the roasting pan. Add 4 litres of water and a bouquet garni (parsley, thyme, bay leaves, crushed pepper and salt). Bring to boil and skim well. Reduce heat and simmer for 3 hours, cool, remove fat from surface and strain through a fine sieve.
Stock can be frozen and used when required. If quick beef stock is required for 4 servings, take 400ml water and use commercial ready made beef boullion to taste.

FISH STOCK

2.5*l* water
1kg bones and trimmings of white
    flesh fish
2 onions, sliced
5 sprigs parsley
¼ teaspoon peppercorns
1 teaspoon salt
juice of ½ lemon

Place all ingredients into a large saucepan and bring liquid to the boil. Skim surface and simmer for 30 minutes. Strain stock through a fine sieve. When cool, stock can be put in containers and frozen and used when required.

VIN BLANC SAUCE

70-80g butter
7 tablespoons flour
2 cups fish stock, seasoned
½ cup white wine

Warm butter, add flour, stir and cook gently (don't discolour). Let cool, then add fish stock and reduce to required thickness and finish off with white wine. Reduce more if required and then beat 2-3 lumps of butter into sauce. Serves 4.

BÉCHAMEL SAUCE (Basic thick white sauce)

70-80g butter
6 tablespoons flour
2 cups milk
½ small onion
3 cloves
1 bay leaf
pinch nutmeg
1 teaspoon salt
¼ teaspoon white pepper

Warm butter in saucepan, stir in flour and cook gently (do not discolour). Remove from heat and allow to cool. Add boiling milk and whisk vigorously. Spike onion with cloves and add to sauce. Add bay leaf, pinch of nutmeg to sauce. Simmer for 20-30 minutes. Strain through fine sieve, season to taste.

CREAM SAUCE

Use Béchamel Sauce and add ½ cup, or more if desired, double cream. Reduce to required thickness and finish off with lemon juice to taste.

BROWN SAUCE or SAUCE ESPAGNOLE

150g butter
150g flour
4.5l brown stock, warm
Mirepoix* 100g carrot, 100g
    onion diced, 75g lean bacon,
    diced
½ cup white sauce
sprig thyme
½ bay leaf
½l tomato purée

Make roux using butter and flour and add 4 litres warm light brown stock. Mix and boil over a brisk heat. Make a Mirepoix of carrot and onion and lightly fry with diced lean bacon. Pour off the bacon fat, dilute the pan juices with white wine, and add to the sauce, together with thyme and bay leaf. Cook the sauce very gently for 2½ hours, skimming frequently. Strain, pressing the vegetables well to extract their juices. Put back in saucepan and add ½ litre stock. Cook for further 2 hours, skimming frequently. Add tomato purée. Mix well, cook slowly for further hour. Remove all grease and strain through fine sieve.
N.B. If sauce becomes too thick, more stock may be added to reach desired consistency.

*MIREPOIX: Vegetables cut, the degree of fineness depending on the use for which intended, cooked in butter with diced ham or bacon.

DEMI-GLACE

Reduce Brown Sauce or Espagnole Sauce until quite thick then add madeira to taste and beat some butter (flakes) into sauce.

MUSHROOM SAUCE

Sauté some sliced mushrooms with a bit of red wine and then add required amount of demi-glace.

MILANAISE SAUCE

300ml demi-glace
1-2 teaspoons tomato purée
3-4 tomatoes, peeled, chopped
   and pips removed
1 clove garlic, crushed
3-4 mushrooms, cut into julienne

Boil demi-glace with tomato purée, add tomato and garlic and mushrooms. Bring to boil and serve.

HOLLANDAISE SAUCE

4-5 tablespoons wine vinegar
2-3 tablespoons water
pinch salt
pinch coarsley ground pepper
5 egg yolks
1 extra tablespoon water
450g butter, melted
2-3 tablespoons water
lemon juice

Boil down by two thirds: wine vinegar mixed with water, pinch of salt and coarsley ground pepper. Let the saucepan cool a little then add 5 raw egg yolks, beaten slightly with a tablespoon of water. Whisk the sauce over a very gentle heat or double boiler. As soon as the yolks thicken to a creamy consistency add little by little, and beating all the time, 450g of lukewarm melted butter. Add another 2-3 tablespoons of water, a few drops at a time. Season and add a few drops of lemon juice. Strain through a fine sieve. Keep warm. Serves 6-8.

BÉARNAISE SAUCE

2 tablespoon chopped tarragon
1 tablespoon chopped chervil
1 tablespoon chopped shallots
pinch thyme
3 tablespoons white wine
3 tablespoons vinegar

Put all ingredients in a saucepan and reduce until all liquid is gone, but do not colour. Add this reduced mixture to Hollandaise Sauce previously prepared. Serves 6-8.

SWEET AND SOUR SAUCE

½ cup sugar
⅓ cup vinegar
½ cup water
1 tablespoon dry sherry
2 tablespoons soy sauce
1-2 tablespoons sesame oil
¼ cup green peppers } cut into
¼ cup pickled onions } bite
½ cup pineapple } size
2 teaspoons cornflour

Mix sugar, vinegar, water, sherry, and soy sauce, bring to boil. In the meantime stir and fry green peppers in sesame oil and add with pickled onions and pineapple to sauce. Thicken with cornflour.

CUCUMBER SAUCE

3 tablespoons mayonnaise
4 tablespoons chopped cucumber
½ teaspoon onion, finely chopped
1 dessertspoon mustard
salt and pepper
paprika

Mix together first four ingredients and season to taste. Good with ham or fish salads.

LOW-CALORIE DRESSING

4 tablespoons tomato juice (or half
   orange and half lemon juice,
   or grapefruit juice)
½ teaspoon onion, finely chopped
1 teaspoon mustard
sprinkling of salt and pepper

Blend ingredients. Further flavouring may be added, for example, 1 tablespoon chopped parsley, mint or green pepper. For green or other vegetable salads.

DEVILLED DRESSING

1 tablespoon horseradish, finely
   grated
2 tablespoons redcurrant jelly
1 tablespoon mustard
juice of a large orange and finely
   peeled twist of orange rind

Mix ingredients and simmer for 3 minutes. Remove orange peel. Serve cold, whisking well before serving. For cold ham or pork salads.

YOGHURT SALAD DRESSING

150ml yoghurt
1 teaspoon each of chopped parsley,
   chives or onion and mustard

Blend ingredients and season further to taste. Celery or garlic salt is good. Chopped cucumber also blends well into this dressing.
This is particularly good for fish salads.

FRENCH DRESSING

1 part vinegar
3 parts oil
salt and pepper to taste

Mix ingredients together. Mustard, garlic, chopped boiled eggs or chopped herbs can also be added according to taste or what the dressing is going to accompany.

REMOULADE DRESSING

1 cup mayonnaise
1 tablespoon gherkins
1 tablepoon capers
½ tablespoon tarragon   } finely
½ tablespoon chervil   chopped
1 boiled egg

Combine all ingredients. Mix and serve. Usually served with hot and cold fish or on salad.

Bouillabaisse and Pistachio Parfait

RAVIGOTE MAYONNAISE

50ml white wine
50ml tarragon vinegar
½ shallot, finely chopped
1 tablespoon chervil
1 tablespoon capers
½ tablespoon parsley
1 cup thick mayonnaise

Make reduction from wine and vinegar and shallot, until all the liquid is reduced (don't burn). Let cool.
Then add chervil, capers, parsley, mayonnaise, season to taste with pepper and salt. Use for salads and as a dressing for cold fish.

Olvera Street, Los Angeles

METRIC CHART

All cup and spoon measurements are based on the Metric Board's measuring sets.

Handy Measures (for flour)	Ounces	Approximate gram to the nearest whole figure	Approximate to the nearest 25 grams	Imperial Measures (pints)	Approximate to the nearest 25 millilitres
2 good tablespoons flour	1 oz	28	25	¼	150
½ cup flour	2 oz	57	50	½	275
¾ cup flour	3 oz	85	75	¾	425
1 cup flour	4 oz	113	125	1	575
1¼ cups flour	5 oz	142	150	1¾	1 litre
1½ cups flour	6 oz	170	175	¼ cup	50
1¾ cups flour	7 oz	198	200	½ cup	125
2 cups flour	8 oz	226	225	1 cup	225
2¼ cups flour	9 oz	255	250		
2½ cups flour	10 oz	283	275		
2¾ cups flour	11 oz	311	300		
3 cups flour	12 oz	340	350		
4 cups flour	16 oz (1lb)	456	450		
5 cups flour	20 oz (1¼lbs)	569	575		

OVEN TEMPERATURE GUIDE

The following chart gives approximate conversions from degrees Fahrenheit to degrees Celsius (formerly known as Centigrade). This chart can be used for conversion of recipes which give oven temperatures in metric measure.

Description of Oven	°F Automatic Electric	Gas	°C
Cool	200	200	95
Very slow	250	250	120
Slow	300-325	300	150-160
Moderately slow	325-350	325	160-175
Moderate	350-375	350	175-190
Moderately hot	375-400	375	190-205
Hot	400-500	400	205-230
Very hot	450-500	450	230-260

Celsius figures rounded to nearest 5 degrees.

GLOSSARY

BAKE BLIND: To bake a pastry shell empty for filling later. Place tinfoil over the base and up the sides of the cooked pastry and weight it down with rice or dried peas to stop the base of the shell rising. When cooked, remove the foil and store the rice or peas in a jar for future use.

BASTE: To pour or spoon liquid over food as it cooks to moisten and flavour it.

BLACK MUSHROOMS (Dried): These are Chinese winter mushrooms, very strong in flavour, one mushroom being equivalent to about 30g tinned mushrooms. Use very sparingly – one or two will give enough flavour to a meal of 4-6 serves.

BLANCH: To heat in boiling water or steam. This can be done for several reasons:
(1) to loosen outer skins of fruit, nuts or vegetables;
(2) to whiten sweetbreads, veal or chicken;
(3) to remove excess salt or bitter flavour from bacon, gammon, ham, Brussel sprouts, turnips, endive, etc;
(4) to prepare fruits and vegetables for canning, freezing or preserving.

BOUILLON: A clear soup, usually made from beef.

BOUQUET GARNI: A bunch or 'faggot' of culinary herbs, used to flavour stews, casseroles and sauces. Usually consists of sprigs of parsley, thyme, marjoram, rosemary, a bay leaf, peppercorns and cloves, tied in muslin.

BUERRE MANIÈ: Equal quantities of butter and flour kneaded together and added bit by bit to a stew, casserole or sauce to thicken it.

BUTTERMILK: A fermented milk product from which fat has been removed in the process of churning.

CHILLI SAUCE: There are two different types of chilli sauce. The Chinese style is made from chillies, salt and vinegar and has a hot flavour. The Malaysian, Singaporean or Sri Lankan chilli sauce is a mixture of hot, sweet and salty flavours generously laced with ginger and garlic and cooked with vinegar. Both types are readily available.

CHINESE HOT SAUCE: Made from red chillies, apricots, garlic and lemon. Substitute Tabasco or chilli sauce.

CHINESE PARSLEY: Similar to fresh coriander but stronger and more distinctively flavoured. Use leaves only and sparingly.

CHOCOLATE FONDANT: Fondant with melted chocolate added, used for icing cakes and other sweets.

CLARIFY:
1. To clear stock or broth by adding slightly beaten egg whites and crushed egg shells and bring to the boil. The stock is cooled and strained before using.
2. To cleanse fat dripping for deep frying by adding water and melting very gently. When cool, the clean fat is removed and the sediment is left at the bottom.
3. To melt salted butter and drain the oil off the salty sediment.

COCONUT CREAM: Emulsified coconut milk, usually available in tins.

COCONUT MILK: Not the water inside the nut, as is commonly believed, but the creamy liquid extracted from the grated flesh of coconuts or from desiccated (shredded) coconut. When coconut milk is called for, do try to use it, for the flavour cannot be duplicated by using any other kind of milk.

CROÛTON: Fried or toasted cubes of bread used as a garnish or topping or accompaniment to soup.

DE-GLACE: After the food has been roasted or sautéed and most of the fat removed, you then add liquid to the pan and scrape the accumulated pieces of cooked food from the bottom and sides, incorporating them into the liquid.

DEMI-GLACE: A strong, reduced brown sauce. Simmer until quite thick and finish off by beating in some madeira and butter flakes.

DUCHESS POTATOES: Pipe potato purée into required shape through forcing bag on to a buttered baking sheet, brush with beaten egg, place in oven to brown. Use as indicated in the recipe.

FAT CHOY: Dried seaweed, available from Chinese grocers.

FISH STOCK (Fumet): A highly concentrated fish stock, made by reducing well-flavoured fish stock. Used to poach fish, fish fillets or fish steaks, and flavour sauces.

FLEURON: Half-moon shaped, baked puff pastry used for garnish. Crescents should be 40-50mm long.

FONDANT: An icing made by boiling sugar, glucose and water, then working mixture on a marble slab until white. It is commercially available in bakery supply shops.

FOO YOO: A white Chinese cheese made from bean curd sauce and fermented in rice wine and salt. Tastes similar to camembert and it is used for seasoning or is served as a table condiment.

GAME SAUCE: Same as brown sauce, but made from game bones. Apply same method as for brown sauce. You may add juniper berries.

GHEE:
(clarified butter)

Sold in tins, ghee is pure butter-fat without any of the milk solids. It can be heated to much higher temperatures than butter without burning and imparts a distinctive flavour when used as a cooking medium. It can be prepared at home by following method: Boil butter very slowly, skimming off all scum until clear and keep boiling until all water has gone. All solid matter can then be strained off.

GINKGO NUT:

The kernel of the fruit of the maidenhair tree, which grows in China and Japan. It has an individual flavour, and is eaten as a nut or used to give its flavour to foods. Usually sold canned.

GLAZE:

A thin coating of beaten egg, syrup or aspic which is brushed over pastry (beaten egg), fruits (syrup) or cooked fish, ham, tongue, chicken, etc (aspic).

HOI SIN SAUCE:

A sweet, spicy, reddish-brown sauce of thick pouring consistency made from soy beans, garlic and spices. Used in barbecued pork dishes and as a dip. Keeps indefinitely in a covered jar.

JULIENNE:

Cut into fine strips, the length of a match stick.

LEMON GRASS:

This aromatic native Asian plant also grows in Australia, Africa, South America and Florida. It is a tall grass with sharp-edged leaves that multiply into clumps. The whitish, slightly bulbous base is used to impart a lemony flavour to curries. Cut just one stem with a sharp knife, close to the root and use about 10-12cm of the stalk from the base, discarding the leaves. If using dried lemon grass, about twelve strips dried are equal to one fresh stem; or substitute two strips of very thinly peeled lemon rind.

MARINADE:

Usually a mixture of an oil, acid and seasonings in which food is marinated to give it more flavour and to soften the tissues of tough food.

MARINATE:

To let food stand in a marinade.

MONOSODIUM GLUTAMATE:

White crystals like coarse salt. Monsodium glutamate is an extract of grains and vegetables with no flavour of its own; it acts as a catalyst on the taste buds to enhance other flavours. If food is of good quality and cleverly seasoned it is not necessary to use this additive. It is also well known under the brand names 'Vetsin' and 'Aji-no-moto'.

NOISETTE:

Small individual portion from lamb, veal etc.

OYSTER SAUCE:

Adds delicate flavour to all kinds of dishes. Made from oysters cooked in soy sauce and brine, this thick sauce can be kept indefinitely without refrigeration.

PARBOIL:	To boil until partially cooked.
PLUM SAUCE:	A spicy, sweet, hot Chinese sauce made from plums, chillies, vinegar, spices and sugar. Use as a dip. It keeps indefinitely in a covered jar.
PROVE:	To let a dough rise in a warm place.
PURÉE:	To press through a fine sieve or put in a food blender to produce a smooth thick mixture.
RED SHRIMP BUTTER:	Pound shrimps and add equal amount of butter. Season with cayenne pepper and a dash of tomato sauce. Used for addition in sauces.
REDUCE:	To cook a sauce over a high heat, uncovered, until it is reduced by evaporation to the desired consistency. This culinary process improves both flavour and appearance.
RICE NOODLES: (Vermicelli)	Sometimes labelled 'rice sticks'. These are very fine rice flour noodles sold in Chinese grocery stores. Soaking in hot water for ten minutes prepares them sufficiently for most recipes, but in some cases they may need boiling for one or two minutes. When deep fried they swell up and turn white. For a crisp result, fry them straight from the packet without soaking.
RICE PILAF:	To make: fry rice in butter (do not allow to colour), add water or any clear stock, bring to boil and then cover and place in oven until cooked approximately 20 minutes. Add butter flakes, stir into rice with fork and serve.
ROUX:	A mixture of fat and flour cooked slowly over a low heat used as a foundation for sauces, soups and thick gravies.
ROYAL ICING:	White icing made from icing sugar and egg whites. To 500g icing sugar add 3 egg whites and beat until creamy.
SAMBAL ULEK:	A combination of chillies and salt, used in cooking or as an accompaniment, the old Dutch-Indonesian spelling, still seen on some labels, is Sambal Oelek.
SAUTÉ:	To fry lightly in a small amount of hot fat or oil, shaking the pan or turning food frequently during cooking, usually until the fat or oil is absorbed.
SCALLION:	Spring onion.
SERAH POWDER:	Same as lemon grass.

SESAME PASTE:

Sesame seeds, when ground, yield a thick paste similar to peanut butter. Stores specialising in Middle Eastern foods sell a sesame paste known as *Tahini*, but this is made from raw sesame seeds, is white and slightly bitter, and cannot be substituted for the Chinese version – which is made from toasted sesame seeds, and is brown and nutty. A suitable substitute is peanut butter with sesame oil added. Sesame paste is sold in cans or jars and keeps indefinitely after opening.

SHRIMP BUTTER:

See Red Shrimp Butter. Same method but excluding cayenne pepper and tomato sauce.

STAR ANISE:

The dried, star-shaped fruit of an evergreen tree native to China, it consists of eight segments or points. It is essential in Chinese cooking.

STOCK SYRUP:

Made by boiling 6 parts sugar, 5 parts water and 1 part glucose. May be kept in an airtight bottle and refrigerated.

TRASI:

Indonesian dried shrimp paste made from prawns. It is sold in cans of flat slabs or cakes and will keep indefinitely. It does not need refrigeration. Commercially sold as 'Blachan'.

WHITE WINE-CHINESE:

Made from rice-like grain which grows in China. Similar to gin or vodka but much stronger. Substitutes are dry or pale sherry, gin or Japanese sake.

INDEX